BEAD JOURNEY

Jewelry from around the world

AFRICA ASIA & THE PACIFIC RIM
THE AMERICAS EUROPE

Kalmbach Books
21027 Crossroads Circle
Waukesha, Wisconsin 53186
www.kalmbach.com/books

Published in 2008
12 11 10 09 08   1 2 3 4 5

Manufactured in
the United States of America

ISBN: 978-0-87116-267-0

The material in this book has previously
appeared as articles in *BeadStyle Around
the World*, with the exception of those
by Jane Konkel on pages 17, 26, 36, 38,
57, 70, 78, and 92. Special thanks to Ms.
Konkel for her ideas and contributions.
BeadStyle is registered as a trademark.

Library of Congress
Cataloging-in-Publication Data

Bead journey : jewelry from around the
world.

   p. : col. ill. ; cm.

  "Africa, Asia & the Pacific Rim, the
Americas, Europe."
   ISBN: 978-0-87116-267-0

1. Beadwork. 2. Jewelry making.

TT860 .B42 2008
745.582

Contents

p. 58

p. 81

p. 37

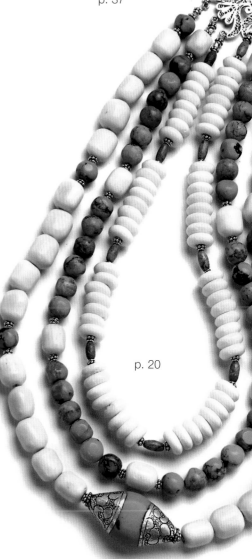

p. 20

Introduction

Everyone needs a bit of a vacation to distract them from day-to-day life, and visiting a new location, whether it's across the street or across the globe, invites us to experience and appreciate cultures that are fresh and exciting to us. But if a trip to another country soon just isn't in the cards, you can still travel around the world without leaving home by learning about and making new jewelry that honors another region. And that's where *Bead Journey* comes in.

Whether you crave the sparkle of Austrian crystals or enjoy the elegance of Chinese cloisonné, *Bead Journey* can guide you through the steps of making a wide variety of necklaces, bracelets, and earrings that are exotic and chic — and symbolic of another country. We've divided the book into four sections: Asia and the Pacific Rim, Africa, Europe, and the Americas. Each section contains a variety of projects that use materials or designs from the region, supplying beautiful inspiration for beaders of all skill levels. New beaders can turn to our Basics section (opposite) to learn all the techniques needed to complete these projects.

The jewelry in this book represents other locations in many different ways. It might be made from beads that are crafted in that country, like Jane Konkel's belt of Ecuadorian tagua beads (p. 78). It might contain gemstones mined in that country, such as the carnelian and jade from New Zealand in Cathy Jakicic's necklace-and-bracelet set (p. 28). Or it might use a traditional image or style, like the Viking-esque skull beads in Tia Torhost's necklace and earrings representing Scandinavia (p. 41). Whatever the connection, it adds a layer of significance to already beautiful jewelry.

So take off on your virtual vacation to 32 different countries with *Bead Journey*!

Basics

A step-by-step reference to key jewelry-making techniques used in bead-stringing projects

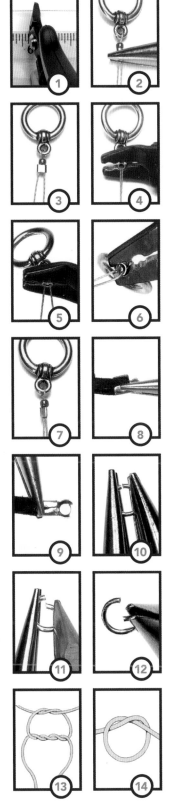

CUTTING FLEXIBLE BEADING WIRE
1 Determine the finished length of your necklace. Add 6 in. (15cm) and cut a piece of beading wire to that length. (For a bracelet, add 5 in./13cm.)

FLATTENED CRIMP
2 Hold the crimp bead with the tip of your chainnose pliers. Squeeze the pliers firmly to flatten the crimp bead.
3 Tug the wire to make sure the crimp has a solid grip. If the wire slides, remove the crimp and repeat the steps with a new crimp bead.

FOLDED CRIMP
4 Position the crimp bead in the notch closest to the crimping pliers' handle.
5 Separate the wires and firmly squeeze the crimp bead.
6 Move the crimp bead into the notch at the pliers' tip, and hold the crimp bead. Squeeze the pliers, folding the bead in half at the indentation.
7 Test the folded crimp.

FOLDED CRIMP END
8 Glue one end of the cord and place it in a crimp end. Use chainnose pliers to fold one side of the crimp end over the cord.
9 Repeat with the second side of the crimp end and squeeze gently.

OPENING A JUMP RING, LOOP, OR EARRING WIRE
10 Hold the jump ring or loop with two pairs of chainnose pliers or with chainnose and roundnose pliers.
11 To open the jump ring or loop, bring one pair of pliers toward you and one away from you.
12 Reverse the steps to close the open jump ring.

SURGEON'S KNOT
13 Cross the right end over the left and go through the loop. Go through again. Cross the left end over the right and go through. Pull the ends to tighten the knot.

OVERHAND KNOT
14 Make a loop and pass the working end through it. Pull the ends to tighten the knot.

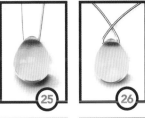

PLAIN LOOP
15 Trim the wire ⅜ in. (1cm) above the top bead. Make a right-angle bend close to the bead.
16 Grab the wire's tip with roundnose pliers. Roll the wire to form a half circle. Release the wire.
17 Reposition the pliers in the loop and continue rolling, forming a centered circle above the bead.
18 The finished loop.

WRAPPED LOOP
19 Make sure there is at least 1¼ in. (3.2cm) of wire above the bead. With the tip of your chainnose pliers, grasp the wire directly above the bead. Bend the wire above the pliers into a right angle.
20 Position the jaws of your roundnose pliers in the bend.
21 Bring the wire over the top jaw of the pliers.
22 Reposition the pliers' lower jaw snugly in the curved wire. Wrap the wire down and around the bottom of the pliers. This is the "first half of a wrapped loop."
23 Grasp the loop with chainnose pliers.
24 Wrap the wire tail around the stem, covering the stem between the loop and the top bead. Trim the excess wrapping wire and press the end close to the wraps with chainnose or crimping pliers.

MAKING A SET OF WRAPS ABOVE A TOP-DRILLED BEAD
25 Center a top-drilled bead on a 3-in. (7.6cm) piece of wire. Bend each wire upward to form a squared-off U shape.
26 Cross the wires into an X above the bead.
27 Using chainnose pliers, make a small bend in each wire so the ends form a right angle.
28 Wrap the horizontal wire around the vertical wire as in a wrapped loop. Trim the excess wrapping wire.

ASIA & THE PACIFIC RIM

For some, thoughts of Asia and the Pacific Rim elicit images of the exotic and the unfamiliar, but these projects are as easy to wear as they are to make. Cloisonné from China, carnelian and jade-colored beads from New Zealand, and pearls from Japan and the South Seas all capture the elegance of the Far East. Wood beads from the Philippines, bone from Nepal, silver from Thailand, lapis lazuli from Afghanistan, and recycled glass from India each add their own distinct spice to the mix.

p.20

p.23

p.8

p.17

CHINA

AFGHANISTAN

NEPAL

SOUTH SEAS & JAPAN

INDIA

THAILAND

PHILIPPINES

p.28

p.26

AUSTRALIA

NEW
ZEALAND

p.14

p.10

p.12

Use Chinese cloisonné beads to make an inventive necklace-and-earring set

by Naomi Fujimoto

A spherical Chinese lantern placed outside a home announces a birth, a marriage, or even an illness or death. Here, open-center cloisonné beads make opulent frames; nestle red, pink, or teal crystals inside, or use Asian materials such as carnelian and pearl. Wear them to herald the important ceremonies in your own life — or, at least, to convey your fashion savvy.

Round beads nestle inside cloisonné donuts.

1 **necklace • a** Cut a piece of beading wire (Basics, p. 5). (This necklace is 15 in./38cm.)
   b String the first hole of a cloisonné bead, a pearl, the second hole of the cloisonné bead, and a spacer. Repeat, stringing three more cloisonné beads with a gemstone, a pearl, and a faceted pearl in the center of each, respectively. Repeat until the strand is within 1 in. (2.5cm) of the desired length.

2 On one end, string a spacer, a crimp bead, a spacer, and a lobster claw clasp. Repeat on the other end, substituting a 2-in. (5cm) piece of chain for the clasp. Check the fit, and add or remove beads from both ends if necessary. Go back through the beads just strung and tighten the wire. Crimp the crimp beads (Basics) and trim the excess wire.

3 String a pearl and a spacer on a head pin. Make the first half of a wrapped loop (Basics) and attach it to the end link of chain. Complete the wraps.

1 earrings • Cut a 3-in. (7.6cm) piece of wire. Make the first half of a wrapped loop (Basics). Cut three 1¼-in. (3.2cm) pieces of chain. Attach each chain to the loop and complete the wraps.

2 String the first hole of a cloisonné bead, a pearl, the second hole of the cloisonné bead, and a spacer. Make a wrapped loop.

3 Open an earring wire (Basics). Attach the dangle and close the wire. Make a second earring to match the first.

SUPPLY LIST

necklace
- **22–24** 15mm open-center cloisonné beads (Planet Bead, 414-273-2323)
- **12–13** 8mm round pearls
- **5–6** 8mm faceted round pearls
- **6** 8mm round gemstone beads
- **26–28** 2mm spacers
- flexible beading wire, .014 or .015
- 1½-in. (3.8cm) head pin
- **2** crimp beads
- lobster claw clasp
- 2 in. (5cm) cable chain for extender, 4–5mm links
- chainnose pliers
- roundnose pliers
- diagonal wire cutters
- crimping pliers (optional)

earrings
- **2** 15mm open-center cloisonné beads (Planet Bead)
- **2** 8mm round pearls
- **2** 3mm spacers
- 6 in. (15cm) 24-gauge half-hard wire
- 8 in. (20cm) chain, 2–3mm links
- pair of earring wires
- chainnose pliers
- roundnose pliers
- diagonal wire cutters

Wood, coco, bone, and horn beads come in a variety of shapes and sizes.

SUPPLY LIST

necklace
- **12–15** 8–10mm beads
- **84–102** 8 x 3mm disk beads
- **12–15** 5–6mm beads
- **2** 16-in. (41cm) strands 5 x 2mm or 6 x 3mm saucer beads
- **7–8** three- or five-hole spacer bars with at least 14mm between top and bottom holes

- flexible beading wire, .014 or .015
- **2** crimp beads
- S-hook clasp with **2** soldered jump rings
- chainnose or crimping pliers
- diagonal wire cutters

earrings
- **2** 8–10mm beads
- **8** 8 x 3mm disk beads

- **4** 5–6mm beads
- **32** 5 x 2mm or 6 x 3mm saucer beads
- flexible beading wire, .014 or .015
- **2** crimp beads
- **2** crimp covers
- pair of earring wires
- chainnose pliers
- crimping pliers
- diagonal wire cutters

Blend four styles of wooden beads in a three-strand choker with an island feel

by Marichelle Limjuco-Lopez

Beads made from natural materials are plentiful in the Philippines, so it's easy for local designers to combine several styles in one coordinated, casual choker. To re-create the tropical look, focus on the relationship between size and texture, varying the colors for contrast.

1 necklace • Cut three pieces of beading wire (Basics, p. 5). (This necklace is 15¾ in./40cm.) On one wire, string: two saucer beads, two disk beads, two saucers, 8–10mm bead, two saucers, two disks, two saucers, 5–6mm bead, two saucers, two disks, two saucers.

2 a String the top hole of a spacer bar.
b Repeat the patterns in steps 1 and 2a until the strand is within 3 in. (7.6cm) of the desired length.

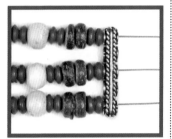

3 Repeat steps 1 and 2a on the remaining wires, stringing the corresponding holes of the spacer bars.
String a spacer bar on the other end of the three wires.

4 On each end of each strand, string two disks and the corresponding hole of a spacer bar.

5 On each end of the top and bottom strands, string four saucers. On each end of the middle strand, string two saucers.

6 On each end, over all three wires, string a saucer, a crimp bead, a saucer, and a soldered jump ring. Check the fit, and add or remove beads from both ends if necessary. Go back through the beads just strung and tighten the wires. Crimp the crimp beads (Basics) and trim the excess wire. Attach an S-hook clasp to one end.

1 earrings • Cut a 9-in. (23cm) piece of beading wire (Basics). String: three saucer beads, disk bead, saucer, 8–10mm bead, saucer, disk, three saucers. Center the beads on the wire.

2 Over both ends, string: two saucers, 5–6mm bead, two saucers, two disks, two saucers, 5–6mm bead, two saucers.

3 String a crimp bead and the loop of an earring wire. Go back through the last few beads strung and tighten the wires. Make a folded crimp (Basics), and trim the excess wire.

4 Use chainnose pliers to close a crimp cover over the crimp bead. Make a second earring to match the first.

A marquise-cut pendant and long earrings give this gaspeite jewelry a streamlined look.

Gaspeite gemstones from western Australia make an eye-catching necklace and earrings

by Andrea Loss

Often mistaken for green turquoise, gaspeite is found in only a few locations and is relatively rare. Australia's aboriginal people hoped using gaspeite would bring them good fortune and success, but even if these cheerful pieces don't bring you good luck, they'll give you great style.

1 **necklace •** Cut a piece of beading wire (Basics, p. 5). (This necklace is 16 in./41cm.) String a round spacer, a gaspeite pendant, and a round spacer.

2 On each end, string three disk beads and a flat spacer. Repeat until the strand is within 2 in. (5cm) of the desired length.

3 On each end, string a round spacer, a crimp bead, a round spacer, and half of the clasp. Check the fit, and add or remove beads from both ends if necessary. Go back through the last few beads strung and tighten the wire. Crimp the crimp beads (Basics) and trim the excess wire.

1 **earrings •** On a head pin, string a spacer, three disk beads, and a spacer. Make a plain loop (Basics). Repeat on an eye pin.

2 Open the head pin's loop (Basics) and attach a loop of the eye pin. Close the loop.

3 Open the loop of an earring wire and attach the dangle. Close the loop. Make a second earring to match the first.

Making this multistrand necklace is easy thanks to consistently sized pearls.

String faux pearls with sparkling rondelles in a three-strand necklace

by Naomi Fujimoto

Known for their luminescence and flawless appearance, Japanese pearls command a hefty price. Make your own necklace, affordably, with shell pearls. These imitations are made in a laboratory, so they are available in consistent shapes, sizes, and colors. You can get gumball-sized pearls that are perfect for this multistrand necklace.

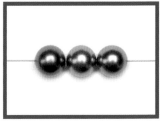

1 necklace • Cut a piece of beading wire (Basics, p. 5). (The shortest strand of this necklace is 15½ in./ 39.4cm.) Cut two more pieces, each 3 in. (7.6cm) longer than the previous piece.

On the shortest wire, center three pearls.

2 On each end of the shortest wire, string a crystal-accent rondelle and three pearls. Repeat until the strand is within 2 in. (5cm) of the desired length.

3 On the middle wire, center seven pearls.

4 On each end of the middle wire, string a rondelle and seven pearls. Repeat until the strand is within 2 in. (5cm) of the desired length.

5 On the longest wire, center five pearls.

6 On each end of the longest wire, string a rondelle and five pearls. Repeat until the strand is within 2 in. (5cm) of the desired length.

7 On each end of each strand, string a spacer, a crimp bead, a spacer, and the corresponding loop of half a clasp. Check the fit, and add or remove beads from both ends if necessary. Go back through the beads just strung and tighten the wires. Crimp the crimp beads (Basics) and trim the excess wire.

SUPPLY LIST

necklace
- 3 16-in. (41cm) strands 12mm round pearls
- 18–22 11mm crystal-accent rondelles
- 12–24 6mm large-hole round spacers
- flexible beading wire, .018 or .019
- 6 crimp beads
- 34mm three-strand clasp
- chainnose or crimping pliers
- diagonal wire cutters

earrings
- 2 12mm round pearls
- 2 11mm crystal-accent rondelles
- 2 10mm accent beads
- 2 1½-in. (3.8cm) head pins
- pair of earring wires
- chainnose pliers
- roundnose pliers
- diagonal wire cutters

1 **earrings** • On a head pin, string a pearl, a crystal-accent rondelle, and an accent bead. Make a plain loop (Basics).

2 Open an earring wire (Basics). Attach the dangle and close the wire. Make a second earring to match the first.

EDITOR'S TIPS

• To lengthen the necklace slightly, string one or two additional spacers per strand before stringing the crimp bead.

• For a variation on the necklace, try stringing the three strands with different-sized pearls and rondelles. The copper-colored necklace shown above uses 86 4mm pearls with nine 5mm rondelles, 62 6mm pearls with four 7mm rondelles, and 45 9mm pearls with six 8mm rondelles.

• Try using 6mm pearls with the 12mm pearls in your earrings rather than accent beads, as in the copper-colored earring pair.

Traditional Indian images strike an exotic chord

The bright hues of the cord and butterfly beads play up the colors of a pictorial pendant.

by Jane Konkel

This handsome pendant is a replica of artwork depicting Indian historical and religious events. Bezeled in sterling silver, the richly colored pendant makes a striking centerpiece for a leather necklace. The stories the pendant tells should inspire your own artistic expression. Recycled-glass butterfly beads from India adorn the leather in the bracelet and earrings.

1 necklace • Determine the finished length of your necklace. (This one is 15 in./ 38cm.) Cut two pieces of leather cord to that length. Over both cords, center a pendant.

2 On each side, over both cords, string three spacers.

3 On each end of each cord, string a crimp end. Using chainnose pliers, flatten the crimp portion of the crimp end (Basics, p. 5).

4 Open a jump ring (Basics). On one side, attach each crimp ends' loop and a hook clasp. Close the jump ring. Repeat on the other side, substituting a soldered jump ring for the clasp.

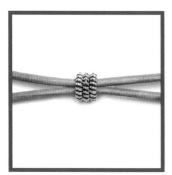

1 bracelet • Cut two 7- to 8½-in. pieces of leather cord. Over both cords, string three spacers.

2 On each cord, string a spacer, a butterfly bead, and a spacer.

3 Over both cords, string three spacers. On each end, over both cords, string a crimp end. Using chainnose pliers, flatten the crimp portion of the crimp end (Basics).

4 Open a jump ring (Basics). On one side, attach the crimp end's loop and a lobster claw clasp. Close the jump ring. Repeat on the other side, omitting the clasp.

SUPPLY LIST

necklace

- 25 x 30mm bezel-set pendant (Jess Imports, 415-626-1433, jessimports.com)
- **6** 6mm large-hole flat spacers
- 2–3 ft. (61cm–.9m) 1.5mm round leather cord (Leather Cord USA, 877-700-2673, leathercordusa.com)
- **4** 1.4mm crimp ends
- hook-and-eye clasp with soldered jump ring
- **2** 6mm jump rings
- chainnose pliers
- diagonal wire cutters

bracelet

- **2** recycled-glass butterfly beads, in two colors
- **10** 6mm large-hole flat spacers

- 14–17 in. (36–43cm) 1.5mm round leather cord (Leather Cord USA)
- **2** 3mm crimp ends
- lobster claw clasp
- **2** 6mm jump rings
- chainnose pliers
- diagonal wire cutters

earrings

- **4** recycled-glass butterfly beads, in two colors
- **14** 6mm large-hole flat spacers
- **4** 4mm large-hole round spacers
- **4** crimp covers
- **1** ft. (30cm) 1.5mm round leather cord (Leather Cord USA)
- chainnose pliers
- crimping pliers (optional)
- roundnose pliers
- diagonal wire cutters

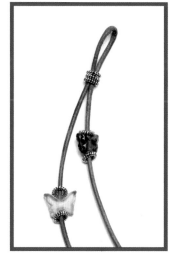

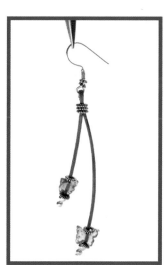

1 **earrings** • Cut a 6-in. (15cm) piece of leather cord. Over both ends, string three flat spacers. Slide the spacers up the cord, leaving a small loop.

2 On each end, string a flat spacer, a butterfly bead, and a flat spacer.

3 On each end, string a round spacer. Adjust the length of the ends so one end is longer than the other. Use chainnose pliers or the first notch of a crimping pliers to close a crimp cover over each end. Trim the excess cord.

4 Open the loop of an earring wire (Basics). Attach the dangle and close the loop. Make a second earring the mirror of the first.

String a necklace and earrings with handcrafted beads

by Jane Konkel

Much of Nepal's jewelry is typical of the jewelry worn in the Himalayan region — a combination of glass, shell, coral, amber, bone, and turquoise. These materials are often worn as amulets to connect the wearer to the spiritual world.

1 **necklace** • Cut a piece of beading wire (Basics, p. 5) for the shortest strand of your necklace. (The shortest strand of this necklace is 16 in./41cm.) Cut two more pieces, each 3 in. (7.6cm) longer than the previous piece.

On the shortest wire, center a spacer, a rice-shaped bead, and a spacer.

2 On each end of the shortest wire, string eight rondelles, a spacer, a rice-shaped bead, and a spacer. Repeat until the strand is within 2 in. (5cm) of the desired length.

3 On the middle wire, center a spacer, a barrel-shaped bead, and a spacer.

4 On each end of the middle wire, string six round beads, a spacer, a barrel, and a spacer. Repeat until the strand is within 2 in. (5cm) of the desired length.

EDITOR'S TIP
To highlight a decorative clasp, wear the necklace off-center.

5 On the longest wire, center a spacer, a Tibetan bead, and a spacer.

6 On each end of the longest wire, string five barrels, a spacer, a round, and a spacer. Repeat until the strand is within 2 in. (5cm) of the desired length.

7 On each end, string a crimp bead, a spacer, and the corresponding loop of half of a clasp. Check the fit, and add or remove beads from both ends if necessary. Go back through the last few beads strung and tighten the wires. Crimp the crimp beads (Basics) and trim the excess wire.

◀ **The focal bead in this necklace was handmade by Tibetan refugees living in Nepal.**

Nepal

1 earrings • On a decorative head pin, string a spacer, a barrel-shaped bead, a spacer, and a rice-shaped bead. Make the first half of a wrapped loop (Basics).

2 Attach the dangle to the loop of an earring post. Complete the wraps. Make a second earring to match the first.

SUPPLY LIST

All turquoise and bone beads are from Happy Mango Beads, happymangobeads.com.

necklace
- 22 x 40mm silver-and-turquoise Tibetan bead
- 16-in. (41cm) strand 11mm bone rondelles
- 16-in. (41cm) strand 10 x 13mm barrel-shaped bone beads
- 16-in. (41cm) strand 10mm round turquoise beads
- 16-in. (41cm) strand 8mm rice-shaped turquoise beads
- **52–58** 4mm spacers
- flexible beading wire, .014 or .015
- **6** crimp beads
- three-strand clasp
- chainnose or crimping pliers
- diagonal wire cutters

earrings
- **2** 10 x 13mm barrel-shaped bone beads
- **2** 8mm rice-shaped turquoise beads
- **4** 4mm spacers
- **2** 2-in. (5cm) decorative head pins
- pair of filigree earring posts with ear nuts
- chainnose pliers
- roundnose pliers
- diagonal wire cutters

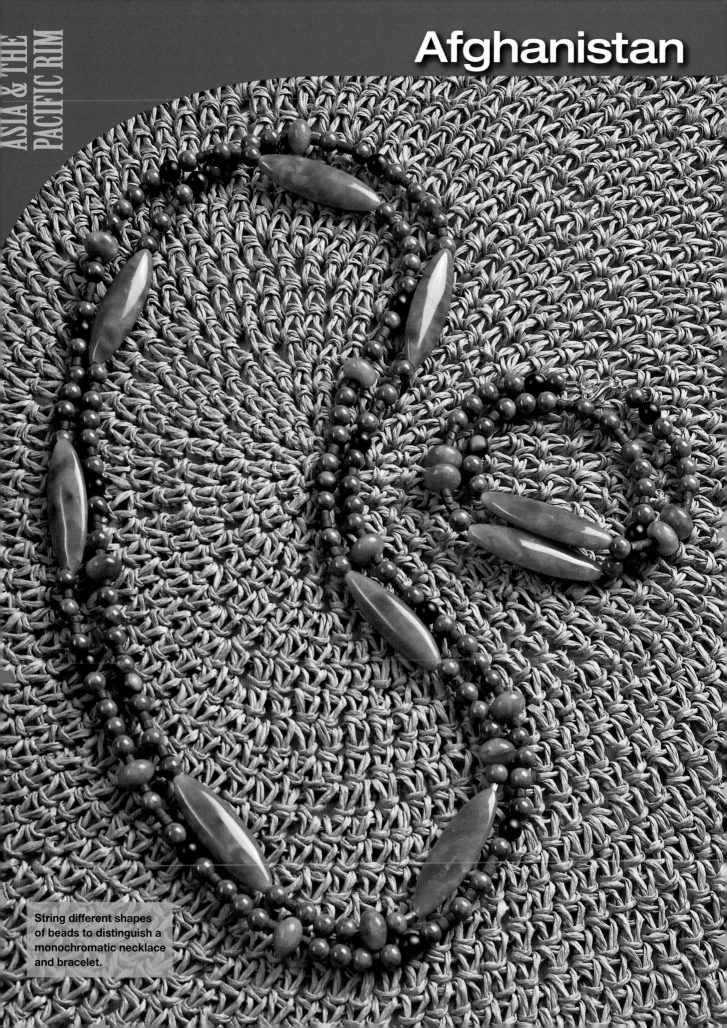

String different shapes
of beads to distinguish a
monochromatic necklace
and bracelet.

A versatile necklace-and-bracelet set mixes glass and quartz with Afghan lapis

by Cathy Jakicic

Lapis lazuli is found in only a few places in the world, including northern Afghanistan, but its popularity is widespread. Ancient Egyptian and Sumerian tombs commonly contain lapis lazuli artifacts, and the stone was often ground for use in paints and pigments in ancient and medieval times. Lapis can be found in shades from very dark to light blue.

1 **necklace •** Cut a piece of beading wire (Basics, p. 5). (This necklace is 46 in./1.2m.) On the wire, center: two heishi beads, 6mm lapis lazuli round, heishi, lapis round, two heishis.

2 On each end, string: lapis round, 6mm round glass bead, lapis round, heishi, three lapis rounds.

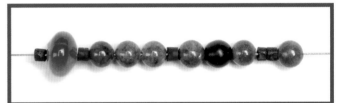

3 On each end, string: heishi, rondelle, heishi, three lapis rounds, heishi, lapis round, glass round, lapis round, two heishis, lapis round. Repeat.

4 On each end, string a heishi, a lapis round, an oval bead, and a lapis round. Repeat steps 3 and 4 until the strand is within 4 in. (10cm) of the desired length.

5 On each end, string: heishi, three lapis rounds, rondelle, lapis round, crimp bead. On one end, string an oval bead. String each end through the last few beads strung on the opposite side, and tighten the wire. Check the fit, and add or remove beads from both ends if necessary. Crimp the crimp beads (Basics) and trim the excess wire.

SUPPLY NOTES

Two 16-in. (41cm) strands of 6mm round lapis lazuli beads and one strand of heishi beads will be enough for the necklace and the bracelet.

SUPPLY LIST

All beads are available from Planet Bead, (414) 273-2323.

necklace
- 7–11 12 x 40mm dyed quartz oval beads
- 10–14 10mm dyed quartz rondelles
- 2 16-in. (41cm) strands 6mm round lapis lazuli beads
- 14–18 6mm round multi-tone matte glass beads
- 16-in. (41cm) strand 3mm lapis lazuli heishi beads
- flexible beading wire, .014 or .015
- 2 crimp beads
- chainnose or crimping pliers
- diagonal wire cutters

bracelet
- 2–3 12 x 40mm dyed quartz oval beads
- 4–6 10mm dyed quartz rondelles
- 26–30 6mm round lapis lazuli beads
- 4–8 6mm round multitone matte glass beads
- 20–30 3mm lapis lazuli heishi beads
- flexible beading wire, .014 or .015
- 2 crimp beads
- lobster claw clasp and soldered jump ring
- chainnose or crimping pliers
- diagonal wire cutters

1 **bracelet** • Cut a piece of beading wire (Basics). (This bracelet is 14 in./36cm.) On the wire, center: two heishi beads, 6mm lapis lazuli round, heishi, lapis round, two heishis.

2 On each end, string: three lapis rounds, heishi, lapis round, 6mm round glass bead, lapis round.

3 On each end, string a lapis round, an oval bead, a lapis round, and a heishi.

4 On each end, string two heishis, two rondelles, and three heishis.

5 On one end, string the pattern from step 2, a crimp bead, and a lobster claw clasp. Repeat on the other end, substituting a soldered jump ring for the clasp. Check the fit, and add or remove beads from both ends if necessary. Go back through the last few beads strung and tighten the wire. Crimp the crimp beads (Basics) and trim the excess wire.

Making silver components has become both profitable and meaningful for Hill Tribe families.

SUPPLY LIST

necklace
- 45mm star-branch pendant (Shiana, shiana.com)
- **8** 3–8mm freeform spacers
- 30g 11º seed beads
- flexible beading wire, .012 or .013
- 6 in. (15cm) 20-gauge half-hard wire
- **6** crimp beads
- **2** 20mm cones

- toggle clasp
- chainnose pliers
- crimping pliers (optional)
- roundnose pliers
- diagonal wire cutters

earrings
- **2** 3–8mm freeform spacers
- 1g 11º seed beads
- **2** 30mm beading hoops
- chainnose pliers

Thai silver spacers shine and complement a handmade pendant

by Jane Konkel

The local Karen artisans who make this pendant are employed by Shiana, a company that specializes in fair-trade jewelry and components. They are paid more than the average minimum wage, and Shiana funds the building of schools and training facilities for the villagers.

SUPPLY NOTES

There are different names for the freeform spacers used in this necklace and earring set. Shiana refers to them as liquid drop beads. They are also available from Fusion Beads (888-781-3559, fusionbeads.com). They refer to the spacers as Thai silver spacers.

1 **necklace** • Cut three pieces of beading wire (Basics, p. 5). (This necklace is 20 in./51cm.) Over all three wires, center a freeform spacer, a pendant, and a spacer.

2 On each side, on one wire, string 1 in. (2.5cm) of 11º seed beads and a spacer. On the second wire, string 2 in. (5cm) 11ºs and a spacer. On the third wire, string 3 in. (7.6cm) of 11ºs and a spacer.

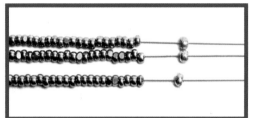

3 On each end of each strand, string 11ºs until the strands are within 2 in. (5cm) of the desired length. Check the fit, and add or remove beads from both ends if necessary. On each end of each strand, string a crimp bead.

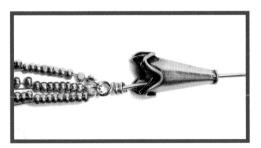

4 Cut two 3-in. (7.6cm) pieces of 20-gauge wire. Make a wrapped loop on one end of each wire (Basics).

5 On each end of each wire, string the wrapped loop. Go back through the beads just strung and tighten the wire. Crimp the crimp beads and trim the excess wire.

1 **earrings** • On a beading hoop, string 11 11º seed beads, a freeform spacer, and 11 11ºs.

6 On each end, string a cone.

7 Make the first half of a wrapped loop above the cone and attach half of a clasp. Complete the wraps. Repeat on the other end with the remaining clasp half.

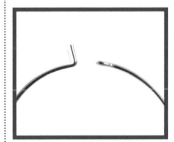

2 Bend the wire upward ¼ in. (6mm) from the end of the hoop. Make a second earring to match the first.

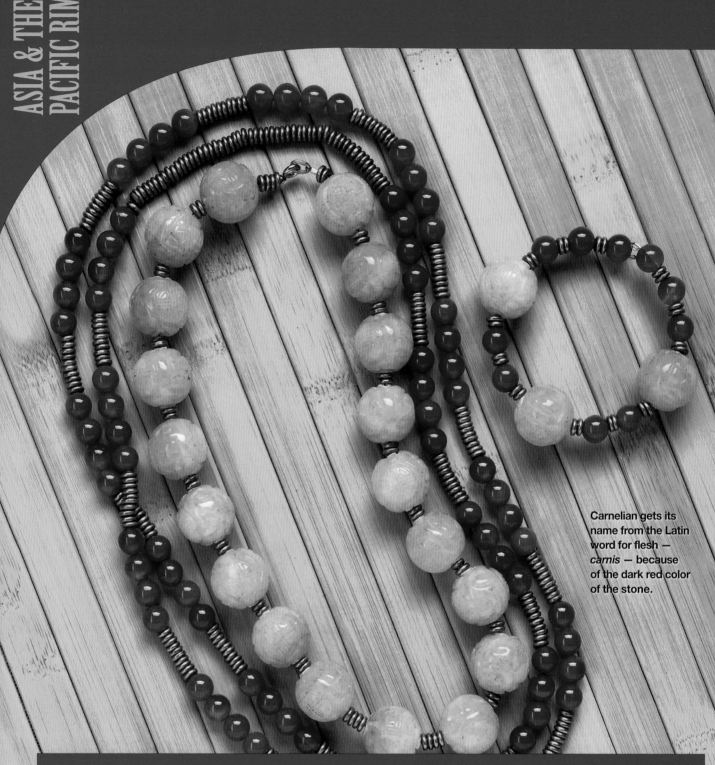

Carnelian gets its name from the Latin word for flesh — *carnis* — because of the dark red color of the stone.

SUPPLY LIST

aventurine necklace
- 16-in. (41cm) strand 18mm round carved aventurine beads (Planet Bead, 414-273-2323)
- **46–54** 5mm flat copper-colored spacers
- flexible beading wire, .018 or .019
- **2** crimp beads

- spring-ring clasp and soldered jump ring
- chainnose or crimping pliers
- diagonal wire cutters

carnelian necklace
- 16-in. (41cm) strand 8mm round carnelian beads
- 16-in. (41cm) strand 5mm flat copper-colored spacers

- flexible beading wire, .014 or .015
- **3** crimp beads
- chainnose or crimping pliers
- diagonal wire cutters

cuff bracelet
- **3–4** 18mm round carved aventurine beads (Planet Bead)

- **10–12** 8mm round carnelian beads
- **24–30** 5mm flat copper-colored spacers
- memory wire, bracelet diameter
- chainnose pliers
- roundnose pliers
- heavy-duty wire cutters (optional)

Carnelian and jade-colored beads give necklaces and bracelet an exotic flair

by Cathy Jakicic

Both carnelian and jade are found in New Zealand: carnelian across the country and jade mainly on the west coast. An accessible substitute for green jade is aventurine, which imitates the color but not the price of its more precious counterpart. These two necklaces can be worn individually or together. String a matching cuff in a matter of minutes.

1 **cuff bracelet** • Separate one memory-wire coil from the stack (see p. 81). Cut the memory wire. Using roundnose pliers, make a small loop on one end.

2 String: carnelian bead, two spacers, carnelian, two spacers, carnelian, two spacers.

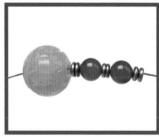

3 String: aventurine bead, two spacers, carnelian, two spacers, carnelian, two spacers. Repeat twice.

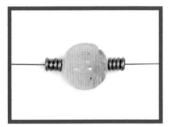

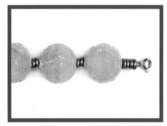

1 **aventurine necklace** • Cut a piece of beading wire (Basics, p. 5). (This necklace is 17 in./43cm.) Center four spacers, an aventurine bead, and four spacers on the wire.

2 On each end, string an aventurine and two spacers. Repeat until the necklace is within 1 in. (2.5cm) of the desired length.

3 On one end, string a crimp bead, two spacers, and a clasp. Repeat on the other end, substituting a soldered jump ring for the clasp. Check the fit, and add or remove beads from both ends if necessary. Go back through the beads just strung and tighten the wire. Crimp the crimp beads (Basics) and trim the excess wire.

DESIGN GUIDELINE

If you prefer a less chunky aventurine necklace, include 8mm carnelian beads.

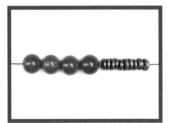

1 **carnelian necklace** • Cut a piece of beading wire (Basics). (This necklace is 42 in./1.1m.) String four carnelian beads and ten spacers. Repeat until the necklace is within 3 in. (7.6cm) of the desired length.

2 On one end, string: crimp bead, 15 spacers, crimp bead, 15 spacers, crimp bead, 15 spacers. Bring the other end through the beads just strung. Check the fit, and add or remove beads from both ends if necessary. Tighten the wires, crimp the crimp beads (Basics), and trim the excess wire.

4 String a carnelian. Trim the memory wire (see p. 81) to ¼ in. (6mm) and make a small loop.

EUROPE

European jewelry is as diverse as the countries that make up the continent. Some projects use components created or mined in a particular area – such as Venetian-glass beads, Austrian crystals, Czech glass, Scandinavian pyrite, Polish amber, or Greek clay. Others use materials, like Victorian-style jet beads from England and pendants portraying faeries from Scotland's folklore, that reflect the history of the country they represent through color or design.

p. 44

p. 46

p. 49

p. 36

SCANDINAVIA

SCOTLAND

ENGLAND

POLAND

CZECH REPUBLIC

AUSTRIA

ITALY

GREECE

p.38

p.32

p.34

p.41

SUPPLY LIST

All filigree beads are from Michaels (michaels.com for store locations).

necklace
• Venetian-glass beads (Via Murano, 949-706-2898, viamurano.com)
  35mm disk
  6 14mm round
  2 12mm round
  4 10mm round
  8–12 8mm round
• filigree beads
  4 10mm round
  10 8mm round
  8–16 6mm round
• 1g 11º seed beads

• flexible beading wire, .014 or .015
• 2 crimp beads
• lobster claw clasp and soldered jump ring
• chainnose or crimping pliers
• diagonal wire cutters

earrings
• 4 8mm round Venetian-glass beads (Bella Venetian Beads, 630-305-8232, bellavenetianbeads.com)
• 2 6mm round filigree beads
• 2 2-in. (5cm) head pins
• pair of earring threads
• chainnose pliers
• roundnose pliers
• diagonal wire cutters

Venetian-glass beads link yesterday's grandeur to today's fashion

by Cathy Jakicic

Sumptuous glass beads have been made in Venice since before the second millennium and continue to be synonymous with the city. In this set, airy filigree accent beads add to the opulence without contributing extra weight to this necklace and earrings.

1 **necklace** • Cut a piece of beading wire (Basics, p. 5). (This necklace is 18 in./46cm.) Center an 11º seed bead on the wire. Over both ends, string a 6mm filigree bead, a 35mm Venetian-glass bead, and a 6mm filigree.

2 On each end, string: 11º, 8mm Venetian, 11º, 10mm filigree, 11º, 12mm Venetian, 11º, 10mm filigree, 11º.

3 On each end, string: 14mm Venetian, 11º, 8mm filigree, 11º, 10mm Venetian, 11º, 8mm filigree, 11º. Repeat.

1 **earrings** • On a head pin, string a Venetian-glass bead, a filigree bead, and a Venetian. Make the first half of a wrapped loop (Basics).

4 On each end, string an alternating pattern of Venetian-glass beads, filigree beads, and 11ºs until the strand is within 1 in. (2.5cm) of the desired length.

5 On one end, string a crimp bead and a lobster claw clasp. Repeat on the other end, substituting a soldered jump ring for the clasp. Check the fit, and add or remove beads from both ends if necessary. Go back through the last few beads strung and tighten the wire. Crimp the crimp beads (Basics) and trim the excess wire.

2 Attach the dangle to the loop of an earring thread. Complete the wraps. Make a second earring to match the first.

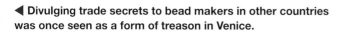

◀ **Divulging trade secrets to bead makers in other countries was once seen as a form of treason in Venice.**

These clay beads come in colors that mirror the splendor of the Mediterranean.

Arrange handmade beads from Athens on a silk cord

by Jane Konkel

The artist who made these beads, Irene Iosifidou, has been making terra-cotta beads for 12 years. She continues to learn new methods for rolling clay and mixing glazes in her Athens home. Her inspirations include the monasteries, the tavernas, and the labyrinth of houses crawling up the cliffs of this port city.

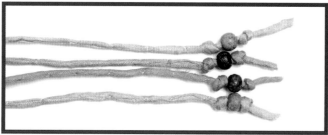

1 **necklace** • Determine the finished length of your necklace. (This one is 41 in./ 1m.) Add 6 in. (15cm) and cut four pieces of silk cord to that length.

String a washer, a 24mm bead, and a washer. Repeat with the remaining beads and washers, positioning them as desired.

2 Approximately 2 in. (5cm) from each end, tie an overhand knot (Basics, p. 5). On each end, string a 6mm bead and tie an overhand knot. Trim the excess cord if necessary.

DESIGN TIP

Change the look of this necklace by spacing the beads at different intervals. Spread the beads along the entire length of the cords, or group the beads at the cords' center. Tie the ends at the back of your neck, or position the tie at the side.

SUPPLY LIST

necklace
- **7–11** 22mm ceramic beads (all beads from Embroidered Soul, 740-965-4851, embroideredsoul.com)
- **14–22** 18mm ceramic washers
- **8** 6mm large-hole ceramic beads
- **4** 37–45-in. (.94–1.1m) silk cords, in four colors
- diagonal wire cutters

earrings
- **2** 20 x 26mm ceramic mini pendants (all beads from Embroidered Soul)
- **4** 6mm ceramic beads, in two colors
- **7** in. (18cm) 22-gauge half-hard wire
- pair of earring wires
- chainnose pliers
- roundnose pliers
- diagonal wire cutters

1 **earrings** • Cut a 3½-in. (8.9cm) piece of wire. String a mini pendant and wrap above it as in a top-drilled bead (Basics).

2 String two 6mm beads and make the first half of a wrapped loop (Basics).

3 Attach the dangle to the loop of an earring wire and complete the wraps. Make a second earring to match the first.

Necklace and earrings show off the size and style versatility of Austrian crystals

by Cathy Jakicic and Jane Konkel

While crystals are made all over the world, the uniform, machine-cut crystals from Austria are considered the gold standard. The wide variety in cuts, colors, and finishes is demonstrated here — though vastly different in size and shape, the crystals in these earrings and necklace are all Austrian.

Daniel Swarovski founded Swarovski Crystals in 1895. He had the factory built in Wattens, in the Austrian Alps, isolated from competitors.

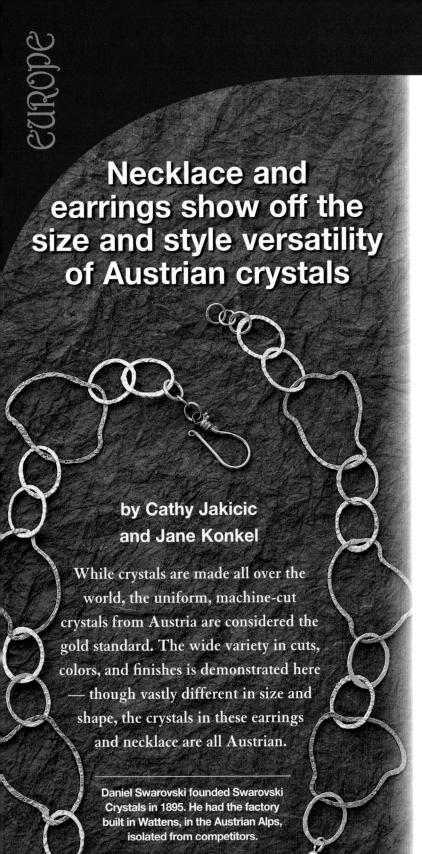

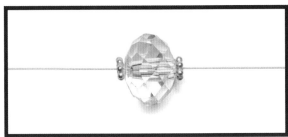

1 **necklace •** Cut a 10-in. (25cm) piece of beading wire (Basics, p.5). Center a 6mm flat spacer, a color-A rondelle crystal, and a flat spacer on the wire.

2 On each end, string a color-B rondelle, a flat spacer, and a polygon crystal.

3 Decide how long you want the chain section to be. (The chain section for this necklace is 14½ in./36.8cm.) Cut a chain to that length, then cut the chain in half. On each end of the beaded strand, string a barrel spacer, a crimp bead, a Wire Guardian, and one chain. Go back through the beads just strung and tighten the wire. Crimp the crimp bead (Basics) and trim the excess wire. Close a crimp cover over each crimp.

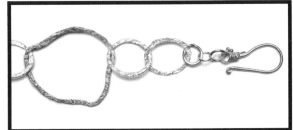

4 Check the fit. Trim links from both ends, if necessary. Open a jump ring (Basics). On one end, attach a chain and a hook clasp, and close the jump ring. Repeat on the remaining end, substituting a soldered jump ring for the clasp.

SUPPLY LIST

necklace
- **3** 18mm rondelle crystals, 1 in color A, 2 in color B
- **2** 12 x 18mm polygon crystals
- **4** 6mm flat spacers
- **2** 5mm barrel-shaped spacers
- **2** 4mm round spacers
- **2** crimp beads
- **2** crimp covers
- **2** Wire Guardians
- **2** 6mm jump rings (optional)
- flexible beading wire, .014 or .015
- 16-in. (41cm) finished chain, 9 and 32mm mixed metal links
- hook clasp and soldered jump ring (optional)
- chainnose pliers
- crimping pliers
- roundnose pliers
- diagonal wire cutters

earrings
- **58** 4mm bicone crystals, color A
- **10** 4mm bicone crystals, color B
- **10** 2-in. (5cm) head pins
- pair of five-hole hoop earrings
- chainnose pliers
- roundnose pliers
- diagonal wire cutters

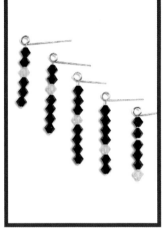

1 earrings • On a head pin, string three color-A bicone crystals, a color-B bicone, and two color-A bicones. Make the first half of a wrapped loop (Basics). Repeat with the following patterns:
- four color As, one color B, and two color As.
- four color As, one color B, and three color As.
- two color As, one color B, and four color As.
- one color B and five color As.

2 Attach the last dangle strung to the first hole on the left of the hoop earring. Complete the wraps.

3 Attach each subsequent dangle as shown. Complete the wraps. Make a second earring in the mirror image of the first.

DESIGN GUIDELINE

Using crystals within the same color family gives a subtle motion to dangles. The earring pictured uses four crystal colors. The first dangle on the left is strung with colors A, B, C, D, A, B, C. The second dangle repeats the pattern, beginning with color B. The third dangle begins with color

C, the fourth with color D, the fifth with color A, the sixth with color B, and the seventh with color C.

Czech glass is available in a wide variety of colors, shapes, and finishes.

Attach a variety of Czech-glass beads for a lush bracelet and earrings

by Jane Konkel

Fire polished, pressed, Picasso — the Czech Republic has a rich history of producing amazing glass beads. Ideal for a bracelet, Czech glass is durable and relatively inexpensive. Explore the possibilities for a bracelet and earrings with these versatile beauties.

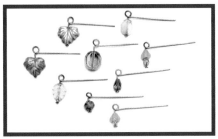

1 bracelet • To make a bead unit: On a head pin, string one or two beads. Make the first half of a wrapped loop (Basics, p. 5). Make 34 to 46 bead units in nine variations.

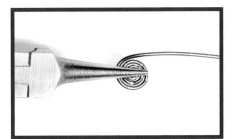

2 To make a coiled-bead unit: Cut a 3-in. (7.6cm) piece of wire. Grasp the end of the wire with the tip of your roundnose pliers and form a small loop. After a complete turn, reposition your pliers and continue to form a spiral.

3 Make a right angle bend with the tail of the coiled wire, string a bead, and make the first half of a wrapped loop. Make seven coiled-bead units. Set one aside for step 8.

4 To make a top-drilled-bead unit: Cut a 3-in. (7.6cm) piece of wire. Make the first half of a wrapped loop. String a top-drilled bead and complete the wraps. String a 3 or 4mm bead and make the first half of a wrapped loop. Make six top-drilled-bead units.

5 Decide how long you want your bracelet to be. Add 1½ in. (3.8cm), for the extender, and cut a piece of chain to that length. Attach a top-drilled-bead unit to the middle link. Complete the wraps.

SUPPLY LIST

bracelet
- 6 14mm Czech-glass beads, top-drilled
- 40–56 3–13mm Czech-glass beads, in nine or more shapes
- 45 in. (1.1m) 22-gauge copper wire
- 6½–8½ in. (16.5–21.6cm) chain, 5–8 mm links (Ornamentea, 919-834-6260, ornamentea.com)
- 40–56 2-in. (5cm) head pins
- lobster claw clasp
- chainnose pliers
- diagonal wire cutters
- roundnose pliers

earrings
- 18 3–13mm Czech-glass beads, in six or more shapes
- 18 in. (46cm) 22-gauge copper wire
- 4 in. (10cm) chain, 3–7mm links (Ornamentea)
- 18 2-in. (5cm) head pins
- pair of earring wires
- chainnose pliers
- diagonal wire cutters
- roundnose pliers

Czech Republic

6 Attach two to four bead, coiled-bead, and top-drilled-bead units to each link, completing the wraps as you go. Do not attach units to the 1½-in. (3.8cm) extender.

7 Cut a 3-in. (7.6cm) piece of wire. Make the first half of a wrapped loop on one end. Attach a lobster claw clasp and complete the wraps. String a 3 or 4mm bead and make the first half of a wrapped loop. Attach the remaining end link and complete the wraps.

8 Attach a coiled-bead unit (reserved in step 3) to the end link of the extender and complete the wraps.

EDITOR'S TIP

Add a twist tie to the chain to indicate your wrist measurement and where the beaded section of your bracelet will be. The remaining chain will be the extender. Before attaching bead units, arrange the large-bead units next to the chain, balancing shapes and colors. Attach the large-bead units first, then fill in with the smaller-bead units.

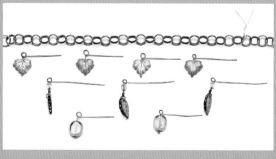

1 **earrings** • Make six bead units, as in step 1 of the bracelet.

2 Make three coiled-bead units, as in steps 2 and 3 of the bracelet.

3 Cut a 2-in. (5cm) piece of chain. Attach a coiled-bead unit to an end link. Complete the wraps.

4 Attach one or two bead or coiled-bead units to every other link, as shown. Complete the wraps as you go.

5 Open the loop of an earring wire (Basics). Attach the dangle and close the loop. Make a second earring to match the first.

Pyrite was named for the Greek word *pyros*, meaning "fire," because hitting pyrite with another mineral or metal causes sparks.

Scandinavian pyrite leaves are the centerpiece of this multitextured necklace

by Tia Torhorst

Pyrite, which is plentiful in Scandinavia, is also called "fool's gold." This necklace uses pyrite leaves along with fire-polished crystals, which are an economical pyrite substitute. Turquoise chips and skull beads that would do any Viking proud complete this necklace-and-earring set.

1 **necklace • a** Unwind 3 ft. (.9m) of thread, leaving it attached to the card.

b Tie an overhand knot (Basics, p. 5) 6 in. (15cm) from the end. String a turquoise chip and tie another over-hand knot next to the chip.

2 Repeat step 1b, inter-spersing fire-polished crystals until the strand is within 1 in. (2.5cm) of the desired length. (This one is 18 in./46cm.) Gently stretch the thread so it doesn't stretch when it is worn.

Trim the thread, leaving 6 in. (15cm) on the end.

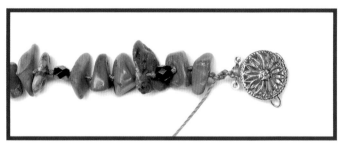

3 Tying several overhand knots, attach one end to the center loop of half of the clasp. Apply glue to each knot. Repeat on the other end.

4 Cut a 3-in. (7.6cm) piece of gold-filled wire. Make a wrapped loop (Basics) on one end. String a crystal and make the first half of a wrapped loop. Make a total of seven crystal units.

5 On each crystal unit, string a pyrite leaf on the loop. Complete the wraps.

SUPPLY LIST

necklace
- 7 15 x 25mm leaf-shaped pyrite pendants (Bead-azzled, beadazzled.net)
- 16-in. (41cm) strand 10–12mm turquoise chips
- 16-in. (41cm) strand 6mm wood skull beads (Beadazzled)
- 3 6-in. (15cm) strands 4mm round fire-polished crystals
- 1g 6º seed beads
- flexible beading wire, .018 or .019
- card of size 8 beading thread
- 21 in. (53cm) 24-gauge half-hard gold-filled wire
- 4 crimp beads
- 4 crimp covers
- three-strand clasp
- chainnose pliers
- roundnose pliers
- diagonal wire cutters
- G-S Hypo Cement
- crimping pliers (optional)

earrings
- 4 10–12mm turquoise chips
- 2 6mm wood skull beads (Beadazzled)
- 2 4mm round fire-polished crystals
- 12 in. (30cm) 24-gauge half-hard gold-filled wire
- pair of earring posts with ear nuts
- chainnose pliers
- roundnose pliers
- diagonal wire cutters

6 Measure the length of the chip strand, add 6 in. (15cm), and cut two pieces of beading wire to that length. On one wire, center five crystals, a leaf dangle, and five crystals.

On each end, string: dangle, five crystals, dangle, five crystals, dangle. On each end, string crystals until the strand is the same length as the chip strand.

7 On the second wire, center a 6º seed bead, a skull bead, and a 6º.

On each end, string an alternating pattern of skull beads and 6ºs until the strand is the same length as the chip strand.

8 On each end of the skull strand, string a crimp bead and the top loop of half of the clasp. Go back through the beads just strung. On each end of the crystal strand, string a crimp bead and the bottom loop of half of the clasp. Go back through the last beads strung. Check the fit, and add or remove beads from both ends if necessary. Tighten the wires, and crimp the crimp beads (Basics).

Using chainnose pliers, close a crimp cover over each crimp bead. Trim the excess wire.

> **EDITOR'S TIP**
>
> Use a stiff wire or needle to move the knots as close as possible to the chips in the necklace.

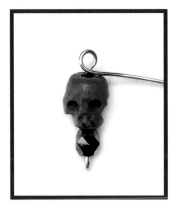

1 **earrings** • Cut a 3-in. (7.6cm) piece of wire. Make a plain loop (Basics) on one end, and string a fire-polished crystal and a skull bead. Make the first half of a wrapped loop (Basics).

2 Cut a 3-in. (7.6cm) piece of wire. Make a wrapped loop on one end and string two chips. Make the first half of a wrapped loop.

3 Attach the skull-bead unit to the wrapped loop of the chip unit. Attach the dangle to the loop of an earring post. Complete the wraps.

Make a second earring to match the first.

Classic chokers pair oversized amber beads with chips or nuggets.

Baltic amber glows in an easy choker and earrings

by Melanie Ehler

Amber is fossilized resin, usually from pines or other conifers. Large deposits are found in the Baltic region. As part of Poland's art and culture since ancient times, amber crafts and jewelry continue to flourish there today. The simple design of this necklace-and-earring duo showcases the rich golds, oranges, and browns that have made amber so highly prized.

SUPPLY LIST

necklace
- **3** 14–20mm round beads or rondelles
- **4** 12–15mm barrel-shaped beads
- 16-in. (41cm) strand 5–8mm chips or nuggets
- **2** 12mm round crystals
- **8–12** 6mm round crystals
- **4** 3mm spacers
- flexible beading wire, .014 or .015
- **2** crimp beads
- lobster claw clasp and soldered jump ring
- chainnose or crimping pliers
- diagonal wire cutters

earrings
- **2** 12–15mm barrel-shaped beads
- **4** 5–8mm chips or nuggets
- **2** 2-in. (5cm) head pins
- pair of earring wires
- chainnose pliers
- roundnose pliers
- diagonal wire cutters

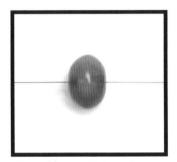

1 necklace • Cut a piece of beading wire (Basics, p. 5). (These necklaces are 15 in./38cm.) On the wire, center a round bead or a rondelle.

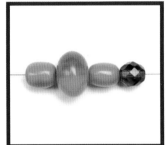

2 On each end, string a barrel-shaped bead, a round or rondelle, a barrel, and a 12mm crystal.

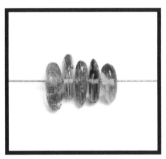

3 On each end, string ¾ in. (1.9cm) of chips or nuggets, using the largest beads from the strand.

4 On each end, string a 6mm crystal and ½ in. (1.3cm) of chips or nuggets. Repeat until the strand is within 1 in. (2.5cm) of the desired length.

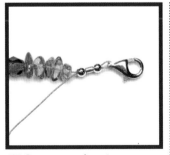

5 On one end, string a spacer, a crimp bead, a spacer, and a lobster claw clasp. Repeat on the other end, substituting a soldered jump ring for the clasp. Check the fit, and add or remove beads from both ends if necessary. Go back through the beads just strung and tighten the wire. Crimp the crimp beads (Basics) and trim the excess wire.

1 earrings • On a head pin, string a chip or nugget, a barrel-shaped bead, and a chip or nugget. Make a wrapped loop (Basics).

2 Open the loop of an earring wire (Basics). Attach the dangle and close the loop. Make a second earring to match the first.

Because jet was rare in France during the Victorian era, "French jet" was developed, made of imported black glass beads from Germany and Bohemia.

Classic styling makes this jet set a tribute to its heritage

by Linda J. Augsburg

Queen Victoria brought jet into vogue when she mourned her late husband, Prince Albert. While the queen dressed in black, her subjects paid their respects by wearing black jewelry. The demand for jet turned Whitby, North Yorkshire, into a thriving mining center. Though jet is still available, faux jet — sometimes called French jet — is more common. Additionally, jet-colored crystals have an opaque coloring and multiple facets that mimic the jet beads from times past.

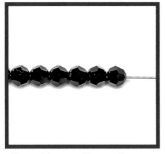

1 necklace • Cut a piece of beading wire (Basics, p. 5) for the shortest strand of your necklace. (This one is 16½ in./41.9cm.) Cut two more pieces, each 1½ in. (3.8cm) longer than the previous piece.

On the shortest wire, center 48 4mm crystals.

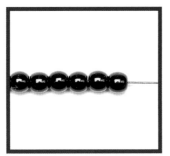

2 On each end, string 4mm glass beads until the strand is within 2 in. (5cm) of the desired length.

3 On the middle wire, center 36 6mm crystals.

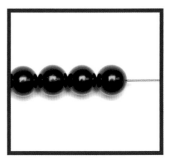

4 On each end, string 6mm jet beads until the strand is 1½ in. (3.8cm) longer than the shortest strand.

5 On the longest wire, string an 8mm crystal, a 5mm bicone crystal, a briolette, and a 5mm. Repeat eight times. String an 8mm crystal. Center the beads on the wire.

6 On each end, string three 8mm crystals. String 8mm jet beads until the strand is 3 in. (7.6cm) longer than the first strand.

7 On each end of each strand, string a 4mm glass bead, a crimp bead, a 4mm glass bead, and the corresponding loop of half of a clasp. Check the fit, and add or remove beads from both ends if necessary. Go back through the beads just strung and tighten the wire. Crimp the crimp beads (Basics) and trim the excess wire.

England

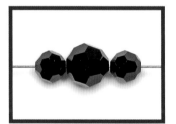

1 **bracelet** • Cut two pieces of beading wire (Basics). On each wire, center a 6mm crystal, an 8mm crystal, and a 6mm crystal.

2 On each end of each wire, string an 8mm jet bead and a 6mm jet bead, repeating until the strand is within 2 in. (5cm) of the desired length.

3 Repeat step 7 of the necklace to finish.

SUPPLY LIST

necklace
- **9** 9 x 11mm black briolettes
- 16-in. (41cm) strand 8mm jet beads
- 16-in. (41cm) strand 6mm jet beads
- **16** 8mm round crystals
- **36** 6mm round crystals
- **48** 4mm round crystals
- **18** 5mm bicone crystals
- 16-in. (41cm) strand 4mm glass beads
- flexible beading wire, .014 or .015
- **6** crimp beads
- three-strand clasp
- chainnose or crimping pliers
- diagonal wire cutters

bracelet
- **16–24** 8mm jet beads
- **16–24** 6mm jet beads
- **2** 8mm round crystals
- **4** 6mm round crystals
- **8** 4mm glass beads
- flexible beading wire, .014 or .015
- **4** crimp beads
- two-strand box clasp
- chainnose or crimping pliers
- diagonal wire cutters

Celebrate Highland folklore with an unusually drilled faerie pendant

Shades of pink, lavender, and amethyst mimic Scottish heather.

by Lindsay Haedt

Fae people, or faeries, play an integral role in Scottish legends. Faeries were considered fickle and unreliable, but the Seelie faeries were also thought to be friendly and benevolent. This necklace features a small faerie — surely of the Seelie court — that rests in the amethyst-hued heather of the Scottish Highlands.

1 necklace • Determine the finished length of your necklace. (This one is 18 in./46cm.) Add 12 in. (30cm) and cut a piece of beading wire to that length. Cut the wire in half. Cut two 8-in. (20cm) pieces of wire.

On each 8-in. (20cm) wire, string a crimp bead, a 3mm spacer, and a bottom wing of the pendant. Go back through the beads just strung and tighten the wire. Crimp the crimp bead (Basics, p. 5). String a 5mm spacer over the crimp. Repeat with each long wire, stringing the top wing instead of the bottom.

2 a On each end, string: 3mm spacer, 6mm rondelle, 8mm rondelle, 6mm rondelle, 3mm spacer, 4mm pearl.

b Repeat once on each bottom strand.

3 On each end, string: 3mm spacer, 6mm rondelle, 8mm rondelle, 6mm rondelle, 3mm spacer.

4 On each side, over both wires, string a crimp bead and an 11º seed bead. With the short wire, skip the 11º and go back through the last few beads strung. Tighten both wires and crimp the crimp bead. Trim the excess wire from the short strand.

On each side, string a 7mm spacer over the crimp.

5 Repeat step 2a until the necklace is within 1 in. (2.5cm) of the desired length.

On each end, string a 3mm spacer, a crimp bead, a spacer, and half of a clasp. Check the fit, and add or remove beads from each end if necessary. Go back through the last few beads strung and tighten the wire. Crimp the crimp bead and trim the excess wire. If desired, close a crimp cover over the crimp.

6 On a head pin, string a 4mm pearl. Make the first half of a wrapped loop (Basics). Attach the pearl unit to the bottom loop of the pendant and complete the wraps.

1 **bracelet** • Cut two pieces of beading wire (Basics).

On each wire, center: 3mm spacer, 6mm rondelle, 8mm rondelle, 6mm rondelle, 3mm spacer.

2 On each end, string: 4mm pearl, 3mm spacer, 6mm rondelle, 8mm rondelle, 6mm rondelle, 3mm spacer. Repeat until each strand is within 1 in. (2.5cm) of the desired length.

SUPPLY LIST

necklace
- 35mm faerie pendant (Green Girl Studios, 828-298-2263, greengirlstudios.com)
- **24–30** 8mm gemstone rondelles
- 16-in. (41cm) strand 6mm gemstone rondelles
- **19–25** 4mm pearls
- **2** 11º seed beads
- **2** 7mm large-hole spacers
- **4** 5mm large-hole spacers
- **54–66** 3mm spacers
- flexible beading wire, .014 or .015
- 1½-in. (3.8cm) 24-gauge head pin
- **8** crimp beads
- **2** crimp covers (optional)
- box clasp
- chainnose pliers
- crimping pliers (optional)
- roundnose pliers
- diagonal wire cutters

bracelet
- **14–22** 8mm gemstone rondelles
- **28–44** 6mm gemstone rondelles
- **12–20** 4mm pearls
- **4** 5mm spacers
- **36–44** 3mm spacers
- flexible beading wire, .014 or .015
- **4** crimp beads
- **4** crimp covers (optional)
- two-strand box clasp
- chainnose or crimping pliers
- diagonal wire cutters

SUPPLY NOTE

One 16-in. (41cm) strand of 6mm gemstone rondelles is enough to make an 18-in. (46cm) necklace and a 7-in. (18cm) bracelet.

3 On each end, string: 5mm spacer, 3mm spacer, crimp bead, 3mm spacer, corresponding loop of half of a clasp. Check the fit, and add or remove beads from both ends if necessary. Go back through the last few beads strung and tighten the wire. Crimp the crimp beads (Basics) and trim the excess wire. If desired, close a crimp cover over the crimp.

AFRICA

The place anthropologists call "the cradle of humankind" is also the birthplace of a wide range of jewelry traditions linked to the people and the raw materials found there. Malachite is mined from the Congo region, and artisans in Ghana make brass beads using the technique of lost-wax casting. Kenyan batik beads, turquoise in an Egyptian design, Ethiopian Coptic crosses, and the jewel-toned gems of Morocco make confining this African art to one simple category impossible.

p.57

p.62

p.65

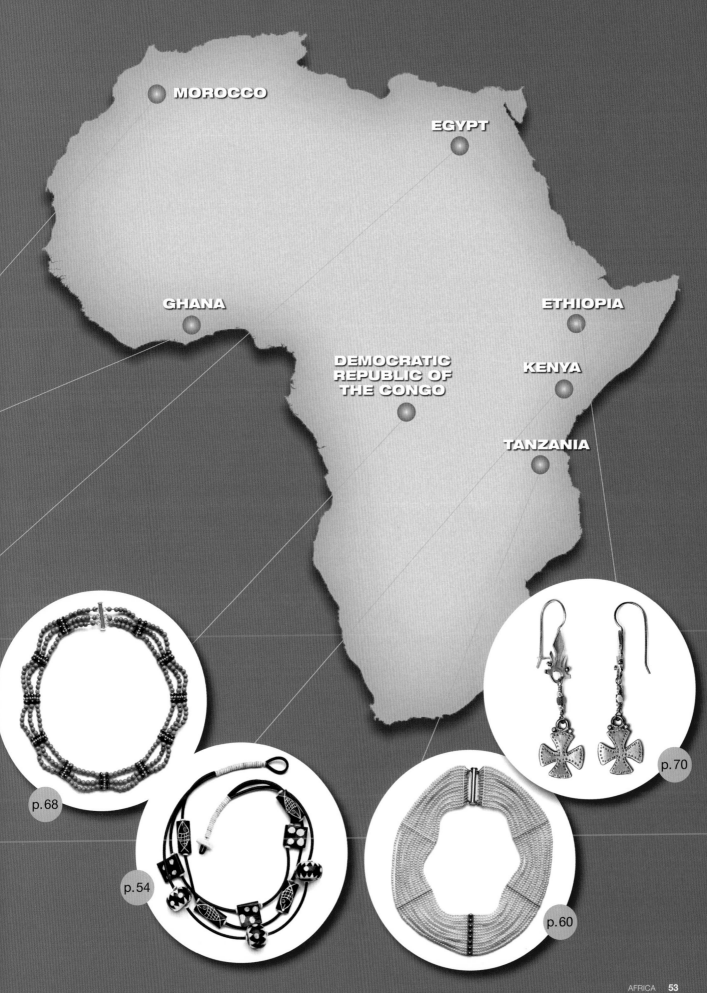

MOROCCO

EGYPT

GHANA

ETHIOPIA

KENYA

DEMOCRATIC
REPUBLIC OF
THE CONGO

TANZANIA

p.68

p.54

p.60

p.70

String batik beads on rubber tubing for a tribal-style necklace and bracelet

by Jane Konkel

When we draw on eggs with crayon and dip the eggs into dye, we're doing a simple form of batik. Similarly, portions of these cow-bone beads from Kenya are coated with wax and stained a dark brown. The wax repels the dye, leaving a pattern on the once-white beads.

SUPPLY LIST

Beads for these projects are available from Planet Bead, (414) 273-2323.

necklace
- **3–5** 25mm round batik beads
- **3–5** 22mm domino batik beads
- 17mm bone disk bead
- **4–6** 14 x 30mm rectangular beads
- 16-in. (41cm) strand 5mm bone spacers
- flexible beading wire, .014 or .015
- 39 in. (.99m) 2.5mm rubber tubing
- **2** crimp beads
- chainnose or crimping pliers
- diagonal wire cutters

bracelet
- 17mm bone disk bead
- 14 x 30mm rectangular bead
- **30–45** 5mm bone spacers
- flexible beading wire, .014 or .015
- 15 in. (38cm) 2.5mm rubber tubing
- **2** crimp beads
- chainnose or crimping pliers
- diagonal wire cutters

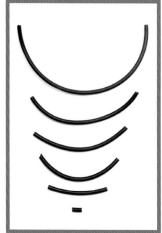

1 necklace • Cut a piece of beading wire (Basics, p. 5) for the shortest strand of your necklace. (This one is 16 in./41cm.) Cut two more pieces, each 2 in. (5cm) longer than the previous piece.

Cut rubber tubing to the following lengths: two 5 in. (13cm), two 3 in. (7.6cm), four 2½ in. (6.4cm), five 2¼ in. (5.7cm), one 1½ in. (3.8cm), one ¼ in. (6mm).

◀ **This necklace and bracelet have unisex appeal.**

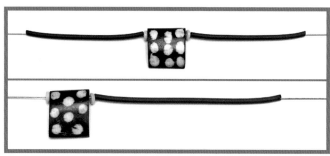

2 a On the shortest wire, center: 2½-in. (6.4cm) tube, spacer, domino bead, spacer, 2½-in. (6.4cm) tube.

b On each end, string a spacer, a domino, a spacer, and a 3-in. (7.6cm) tube.

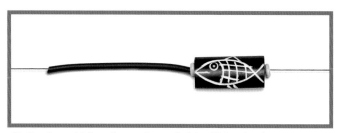

3 On the middle wire, string a 2¼-in. (5.7cm) tube, a spacer, a rectangle bead, and a spacer. Repeat three times. String a 2¼-in. (5.7cm) tube.

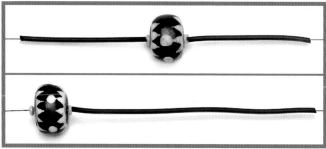

4 a On the longest wire, center: 2½-in. (6.4cm) tube, spacer, round bead, spacer, 2½-in. (6.4cm) tube.

b On each end, string a spacer, a round, a spacer, and a 5-in. (13cm) tube.

EDITOR'S TIP

Clean batik beads with an old toothbrush and mild dishwashing detergent before stringing.

Kenya

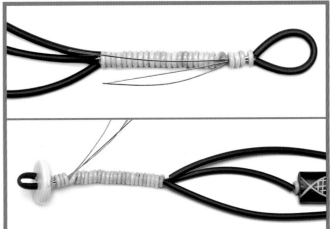

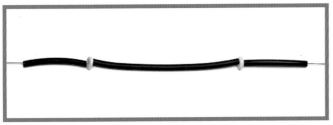

5 On each side, over all three wires, string spacers until the necklace is within 1 in. (2.5cm) of the desired length. Check the fit, allowing 1 in. (2.5cm) for finishing. Add or remove beads from each end, if necessary.

6 On one side, over all three wires, string a crimp bead, a spacer, and a 1½-in. (3.8cm) tube. Go back through the last few beads strung. On the other side, over all three wires, string a crimp bead, a spacer, a disk bead, and a ¼-in. (6mm) tube. Go back through the last few beads strung. On both ends, tighten the wires, crimp the crimp beads (Basics), and trim the excess wire.

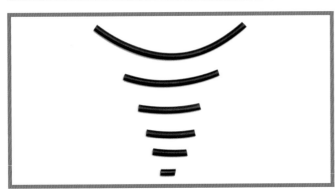

1 bracelet • Cut three pieces of beading wire (Basics). Cut pieces of rubber tubing to the following lengths: one 2½ in. (6.4cm), one 1½ in. (3.8cm), four 1 in. (2.5cm), two ¾ in. (1.9cm), nine ½ in. (1.3cm), one ¼ in. (6mm).

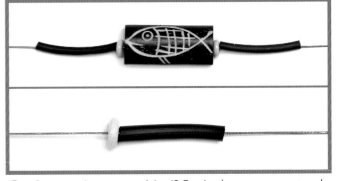

2 a On one wire, center: 1-in. (2.5cm) tube, spacer, rectangle bead, spacer, 1-in. (2.5cm) tube.
b On each end, string a spacer and a ¾-in. (1.9cm) tube.

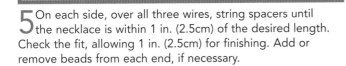

3 On another wire, center: 1-in. (2.5cm) tube, spacer, 2½-in. (6.4cm) tube, spacer, 1-in. (2.5cm) tube.

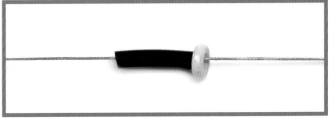

4 On the remaining wire, string a ½-in. (1.3cm) tube and a spacer. Repeat seven times. String a ½-in. (1.3cm) tube. Finish as in step 6 of the necklace.

Ghana

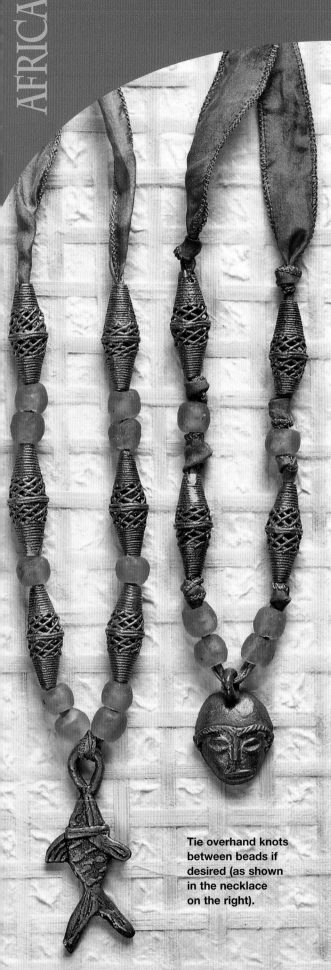

Partner traditional brass with ribbon or leather cord for two necklace styles

by Jane Konkel

To make coiled brass beads, craftsmen in Kurofrum, Ghana, use the lost-wax process of casting, which dates back to the ninth century. Beeswax is formed into an intricate shape, then covered with layers of mud and coconut fiber. Discarded brass is melted down and poured into the mold, displacing the wax. Because each bead is handmade, no two are identical.

1 ribbon necklace • Center a pendant on a ribbon. If the pendant has a parallel loop, tie an overhand knot (Basics, p. 5) to attach the pendant.

2 On each end, string two glass beads, a brass bead, a glass bead, and a brass bead. String additional beads as desired. Trim the ribbon ends to the desired length. (The mask-pendant necklace is 32 in./81cm; the fish-pendant necklace is 39 in./.99m.) Tie an overhand knot to clasp.

Tie overhand knots between beads if desired (as shown in the necklace on the right).

SUPPLY NOTES

Brass beads, pendants, and recycled-glass beads are available from eShopAfrica (eshopafrica.com), Happy Mango Beads (happymangobeads.com), Planet Bead (414-273-2323), and Rings & Things (800-366-2156, rings-things.com).

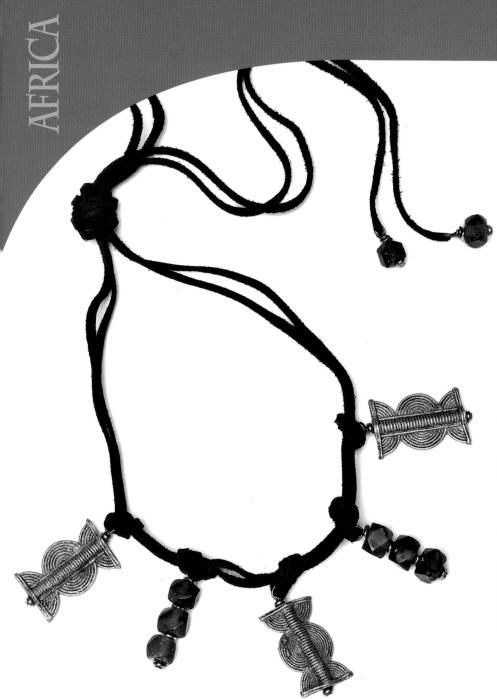

1 **suede cord necklace** • On a head pin, string a spacer, a brass bead, and a spacer. Using the large part of your roundnose pliers, make a plain loop (Basics). Make three brass-bead units.

2 On a head pin, string: spacer, glass bead, spacer, glass bead, spacer, glass bead, spacer. Using the large part of your roundnose pliers, make a plain loop. Make two long glass-bead units.

3 Cut two pieces of suede cord. (This necklace is 48 in./ 1.2m.) Center a brass-bead unit over both cords. Tie an overhand knot (Basics) over the loop of the brass-bead unit.

4 **a** On each end over both cords, string a long glass-bead unit. Position the unit 1 in. (2.5cm) from the previous unit. Tie an overhand knot (Basics) over the loop of the long glass-bead unit.
  b Repeat step 4a with a brass-bead unit.

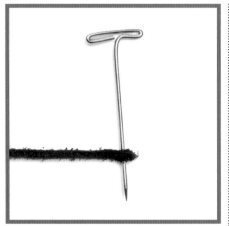

5 On a head pin, string a spacer, a glass bead, and a spacer. Make the first half of a wrapped loop (Basics). Make four short glass-bead units.

6 Using a pin or thumbtack, pierce a hole approximately ⅛ in. (3mm) from each end of each cord.

7 String a short glass-bead unit through each pierced hole, and complete the wraps.

1 earrings • On a head pin, string a spacer, a brass bead, and a spacer. Make a plain loop (Basics).

SUPPLY LIST

ribbon necklace
- 35–60mm brass pendant
- 4–6 33mm lost-wax brass beads
- 6–10 9mm large-hole recycled-glass beads
- 34–46 in. (86–117cm) dyed silk ribbon

suede cord necklace
- 3 28mm brass trade beads
- 10 9mm recycled glass beads
- 22 4mm spacers
- 2 44–52-in. (1.1–1.3m) pieces 3mm suede cord

- 9 2½-in. (6.4cm) head pins
- chainnose pliers
- roundnose pliers
- diagonal wire cutters
- pin or thumbtack

earrings
- 2 28mm brass beads
- 4 4mm spacers
- 2 2½-in. (6.4cm) head pins
- pair of lever-back earring wires
- chainnose pliers
- roundnose pliers
- diagonal wire cutters

2 Open the loop of an earring wire (Basics). Attach the dangle and close the loop. Make a second earring to match the first.

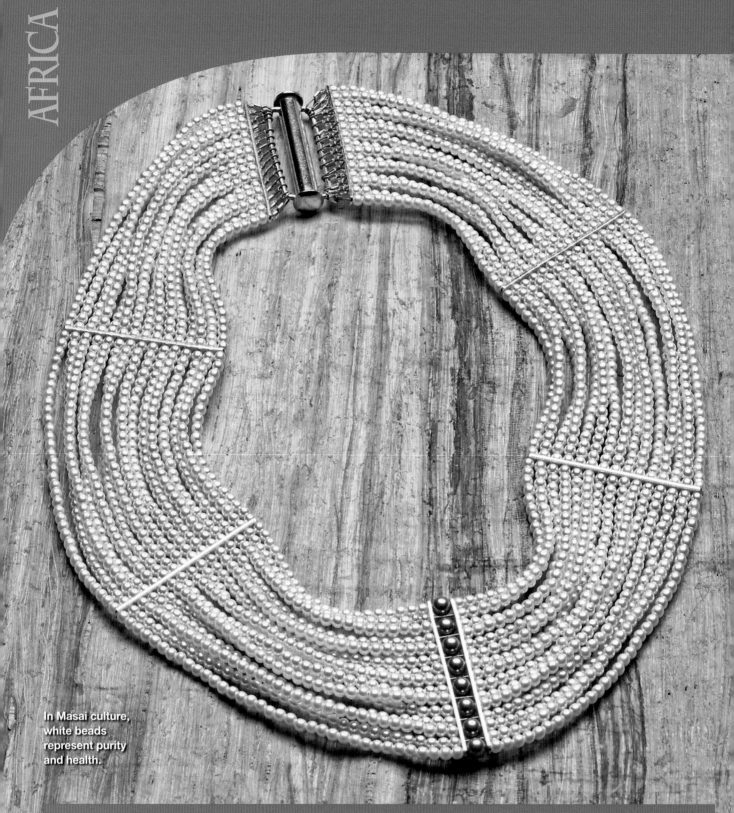

In Masai culture, white beads represent purity and health.

SUPPLY LIST

necklace
- **8** 4mm glass pearls
- **10** 28-in. (71cm) strands 2mm white glass pearls (Rio Grande, 800-545-6566)
- **1g** 11º Japanese cylinder beads
- **8** 38mm 15-hole spacer bars (Rio Grande)
- flexible beading wire, .012 or .013
- **30** crimp beads
- **34mm** slide clasp (Rio Grande)

- chainnose pliers
- diagonal wire cutters

earrings
- **2** 4mm glass pearls
- **8** 2mm white glass pearls (Rio Grande)

- **2** 2-in. (5cm) head pins
- pair of earring threads
- chainnose pliers
- roundnose pliers
- diagonal wire cutters

This Masai-inspired collar pairs traditional form with unexpected materials

by Cathy Jakicic

Women of the Masai tribe of Tanzania wear a variety of beaded jewelry, including multistrand collars. This version uses tiny glass pearls instead of multicolored beads. Delicate pearl earrings accent the collar.

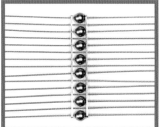

1 necklace • Cut a piece of beading wire (Basics, p. 5) for your shortest strand. (This one is 13 in./33cm.) Cut 14 more pieces, each 1 in. (2.5cm) longer than the previous piece. On each wire, center one hole of a spacer bar, a 4mm pearl, and one hole of a spacer bar, omitting the pearl on every other wire.

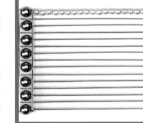

2 On each end of the top strand, string 2mm pearls to one-sixth of the desired length of the strand.

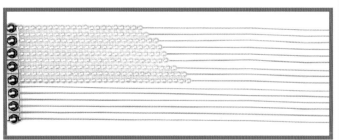

3 On each end of the second strand, string one more 2mm pearl than on the first strand. String 2mm pearls on the remaining strands, adding one more pearl to each strand.

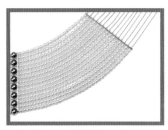

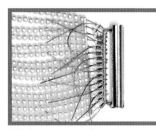

4 a On each side, string a spacer bar over the corresponding strands.
   b Repeat steps 2, 3, and 4a twice.

5 On each end, string a cylinder bead, a crimp bead, and half of a clasp. Check the fit, and add or remove beads from both ends if necessary. Go back through the beads just strung and tighten the wires. Flatten each crimp (Basics) and trim the excess wire.

1 earrings • On a head pin, string a 4mm pearl and four 2mm pearls. Make the first half of a wrapped loop (Basics).

2 Attach the dangle to the loop of an earring thread. Complete the wraps. Make a second earring to match the first.

Combine jewel-toned
gemstones with gold in
a three-strand necklace.

String brilliant Moroccan colors in a gemstone necklace and earrings

by Naomi Fujimoto

Reminiscent of tea glasses and lanterns in a Marrakech bazaar, beads in deep hues make a colorful three-strand necklace. Combine these faceted gemstones with brushed gold accents for your own Moroccan import.

1 **necklace •** Cut a piece of beading wire (Basics, p. 5) for the shortest strand of your necklace. (This one is 14 in./36cm.) Cut two more pieces, each 1½ in. (3.8cm) longer than the previous piece.

On the shortest wire, string garnet briolettes until the strand is within 1 in. (2.5cm) of the desired length.

2 On the middle wire, center three kyanite beads.

3 On each end of the middle strand, string a 3mm spacer and three kyanites. Repeat until the strand is within 1 in. (2.5cm) of the desired length.

4 Cut a 3-in. (7.6cm) piece of 24- or 26-gauge wire. String an amethyst briolette and make a set of wraps above it (Basics). String a 5mm spacer and make a wrapped loop (Basics) perpendicular to the briolette.

DESIGN GUIDELINE

If you substitute other gemstones for the amethyst, garnet, or kyanite, string the largest beads on the longest strand.

5 On the longest wire, center the pendant and a 2mm spacer.

6 On each end of the longest strand, string: 5mm spacer, gold accent bead, 5mm spacer, oval amethyst bead, 5mm spacer, oval, 5mm spacer, oval. Repeat until the strand is within 1 in. (2.5cm) of the desired length.

7 On each end, string a 3mm spacer, a crimp bead, a 3mm spacer, and half of a clasp. Check the fit, and add or remove beads from both ends if necessary. Go back through the beads just strung and tighten the wire. Crimp the crimp beads (Basics) and trim the excess wire.

Morocco

1 **earrings** • Cut a 4-in. (10cm) piece of wire. String a briolette and make a set of wraps above it (Basics).

2 String: 2mm spacer, oval amethyst bead, 5mm spacer, kyanite bead, 2mm spacer. Make a wrapped loop (Basics).

3 Open the loop of an earring wire (Basics). Attach the dangle and close the loop. Make a second earring to match the first.

SUPPLY LIST

necklace
- amethyst briolette, approximately 20mm
- 16-in. (41cm) strand 8–10mm faceted oval amethyst beads
- 16-in. (41cm) strand 6–9mm faceted oval kyanite beads
- **2** 8-in. (20cm) strands 5–7mm garnet briolettes
- **8–10** gold oval beads, approximately 7 x 16mm
- **27–31** 5mm spacers
- **24–28** 3mm spacers
- 2mm round spacer
- flexible beading wire, .014 or .015
- 3 in. (7.6cm) 24- or 26-gauge wire
- **6** crimp beads
- toggle clasp
- chainnose pliers
- roundnose pliers
- diagonal wire cutters
- crimping pliers (optional)

earrings
- **2** 8–10mm faceted oval amethyst beads
- **2** 6–9mm faceted oval kyanite beads
- **2** 5–7mm garnet briolettes
- **2** 5mm spacers
- **4** 2mm spacers
- 8 in. (20cm) 26-gauge half-hard wire
- pair of earring wires
- chainnose pliers
- roundnose pliers
- diagonal wire cutters

Egypt

Unearth
the spirit
of ancient
Egypt with
a turquoise-
and-crystal
necklace

Red or blue
crystals highlight
the matrix pattern in
turquoise cabochons.

by Michael Bellomo

Turquoise was considered one of ancient Egypt's most-prized stones and was often inlaid with carnelian or lapis lazuli in jewelry. Artisans also incorporated red or blue glass to create pieces based on symmetry and pattern repetition. This easy necklace emulates an ancient Egyptian design approach.

EDITOR'S TIP

If the hole of a 2mm silver bead is too small for the beading wire to pass through twice, place the bead on the tip of one jaw of your roundnose pliers. Twist the pliers gently a couple of times to enlarge the hole.

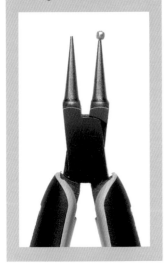

SUPPLY NOTE

The necklace on p. 65 has Swarovski crystals in Indian red. The necklace on p. 67 has crystals in dark sapphire.

1 necklace • Apply Barge cement to the back of a large cabochon and to a beaver-tail finding. Allow the cement to set for a few minutes, and then press the pieces firmly together. Repeat with small cabochons. Allow all pieces to dry overnight.

2 Cut a piece of beading wire (Basics, p. 5). (These necklaces are 15½ in./39.4cm.) Center the large cabochon on the wire with a 2mm bead between the bail's two loops.

3 On each end, string a 2mm bead, two bicone crystals, and a small cabochon with a 2mm bead between the bail's loops.

4 On each end, string three bicones and a small cabochon with a 2mm bead between the bail's loops. Repeat 9 to 11 times.

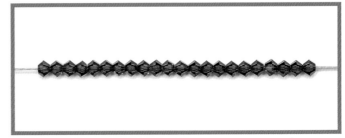

5 On each end, string bicones until the strand is within 1 in. (2.5cm) of the desired length.

6 On each end, string a 2mm bead, a crimp bead, a 2mm bead, and half of a clasp. Check the fit, and add or remove beads from both ends if necessary. Go back through the beads just strung and tighten the wire. Crimp the crimp beads (Basics) and trim the excess wire.

necklace
- turquoise cabochon, approximately 20 x 30mm (Fire Mountain Gems, 800-355-2137, firemountaingems.com)
- **22–26** 6–8mm turquoise cabochons (Fire Mountain Gems)
- **130–160** 3mm bicone crystals
- **29–33** 2mm silver beads
- **23–27** 11mm beaver-tail findings (The Beadiak, 818-597-8020, beadiak.com)
- flexible beading wire, .014 or .015
- **2** crimp beads
- toggle clasp
- chainnose or crimping pliers
- diagonal wire cutters
- Barge cement

earrings
- **2** 6–8mm turquoise cabochons (Fire Mountain Gems)
- **6** 3mm bicone crystals
- **2** 11mm beaver-tail findings (The Beadiak)
- **6** 1-in. (2.5cm) head pins
- **2** 5mm jump rings
- pair of earring wires
- chainnose pliers
- roundnose pliers
- diagonal wire cutters
- Barge cement

1 **earrings** • Apply Barge cement to the back of a cabochon and to a beaver-tail finding. Allow the cement to set for a few minutes, and then press the pieces firmly together. Repeat. Allow the pieces to dry overnight.

2 Open a jump ring (Basics). Attach a cabochon and close the jump ring.

3 String a bicone crystal on a head pin. Make a plain loop (Basics). Make a total of three crystal units.

4 Open an earring wire (Basics). Attach the crystal units and the jump ring. Close the wire. Make a second earring to match the first.

Malachite is believed to heal and protect those who wear it.

SUPPLY LIST

necklace
- **66–78** 5mm faceted rondelles
- **3** 16-in. (41cm) strands 4mm round malachite beads
- **11–13** 5 x 15mm three-hole spacer bars

- flexible beading wire, .014 or .015
- **6** crimp beads
- three-strand slide clasp
- chainnose or crimping pliers
- diagonal wire cutters

bracelet
- **24** 5mm faceted rondelles
- **2** 16-in. (41cm) strands 4mm round malachite beads
- **3–5** 5 x 15mm three-hole spacer bars

- flexible beading wire, .014 or .015
- **6** crimp beads
- three-strand slide clasp
- chainnose or crimping pliers
- diagonal wire cutters

Encircle your neck and wrist with three strands of African malachite

by Andrea Loss

Rich green malachite is found around the world, including in the mines of the Democratic Republic of the Congo. Larger beads are often banded with black. This design should be worn snugly at the base of the neck; a three-strand bracelet completes this regal look.

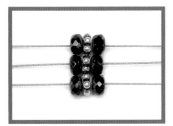

1 necklace • a Cut a piece of beading wire (Basics, p. 5) for the shortest strand of your necklace. (This one is 15 in./38cm.) Cut two more pieces, each 1 in. (2.5cm) longer than the previous piece.

b On each wire, center a rondelle, the corresponding hole of a three-hole spacer bar, and a rondelle.

2 On each end of the shortest strand, string six round beads, a rondelle, the top hole of a three-hole spacer bar, and a rondelle. Repeat the pattern until the strand is within 4 in. (10cm) of the desired length, ending with six rounds.

String a rondelle, the top hole of a three-hole spacer bar, a rondelle, and four rounds.

3 On each end of the middle strand, string seven rounds, a rondelle, the middle hole of a three-hole spacer bar, and a rondelle. Repeat the pattern until the strand is within 4 in. (10cm) of the desired length, ending with seven rounds.

String a rondelle, the middle hole of a three-hole spacer bar, a rondelle, and five rounds.

4 On each end of the longest strand, string eight rounds, a rondelle, the bottom hole of a three-hole spacer bar, and a rondelle. Repeat the pattern until the strand is within 4 in. (10cm) of the desired length, ending with eight rounds.

String a rondelle, the bottom hole of a three-hole spacer bar, a rondelle, and six rounds.

5 On each end, string a crimp bead, a round, and the corresponding loop of half of a clasp. Check the fit, and add or remove beads from both ends if necessary. Go back through the last few beads strung and tighten the wire. Crimp the crimp beads (Basics) and trim the excess wire.

1 bracelet • a Cut three pieces of beading wire (Basics). Repeat step 1b of the necklace.

b On each end, string eight round beads, a rondelle, the respective hole of a three-hole spacer bar, and a rondelle. String rounds until the strands are within 2 in. (5cm) of the desired length. End with a rondelle.

2 On each end, string a round, a crimp bead, a round, and the corresponding loop of half of a clasp. Check the fit, and add or remove beads from both ends if necessary. Go back through the last few beads strung and tighten the wire. Crimp the crimp beads (Basics) and trim the excess wire.

The design of Ethiopian
or Coptic crosses is
often unique to the
regions or towns
where they are created.

SUPPLY NOTE

The brass crosses, tubes, 3mm spacers, head pins, toggle
clasp, and earring wires are from Rishashay, 800-517-3311. The
silver-colored crosses, 8mm accent beads, and 4mm spacers
are from Rings & Things, 800-366-2156, rings-things.com.

Combine Coptic crosses with accent beads

by Jane Konkel

Ethiopian or Coptic crosses have played a major role in religious, cultural, and social life for over 1,600 years. Hinges were introduced into the design in the 19th century by Europeans. Christian Ethiopians wear crosses around their necks as a symbol of faith, while others wear them simply as artistic emblems.

1 **necklace** • On a decorative head pin, string a 2mm spacer, a tube, and a 2mm. Make a wrapped loop (Basics, p. 5). Make six bead units.

2 Cut a piece of beading wire (Basics). (This necklace is 16½ in./41.9cm.) Center an 8mm bead, a brass cross, and an 8mm on the wire.

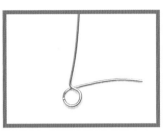

1 **earrings** • Cut a 2-in. (5cm) piece of wire. Make the first half of a wrapped loop (Basics) on one end.

2 Attach a cross and complete the wraps.

3 On each end, string: tube, 8mm, silver cross, 8mm, tube, 8mm.

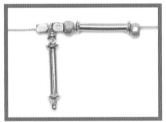

4 On each end, string: 3mm, bead unit, 3mm, 4mm spacer, tube, 4mm. Repeat two times.

3 On the wire, string a 2mm spacer, a 3mm spacer, and a 2mm. Make the first half of a wrapped loop.

4 Attach a decorative earring wire and complete the wraps. Make a second earring to match the first.

5 On each end, alternate stringing tubes and 4mms until the strand is within 1 in. (2.5cm) of the desired length. End with a 4mm.

6 On each end, string a 2mm, a crimp bead, a 2mm, and half of a clasp. Check the fit, and add or remove beads from both ends if necessary. Go back through the last few beads and tighten the wire. Crimp the crimp bead (Basics) and trim the excess wire.

SUPPLY LIST

necklace
- 23 x 30mm brass Ethiopian cross
- 2 16 x 26mm silver hinged crosses
- 22–26 13 x 3mm brass tubes
- 8 8mm silver accent beads
- 18–22 4mm silver spacers
- 16 3mm faceted-brass spacers
- 12 2mm faceted-silver spacers
- flexible beading wire, .014 or .015
- 6 1½-in. (3.8cm) decorative-brass head pins
- 2 crimp beads
- toggle clasp

- chainnose pliers
- roundnose pliers
- diagonal wire cutters
- crimping pliers (optional)

earrings
- 2 19mm brass crosses
- 16 3mm faceted-brass spacers
- 12 2mm faceted-silver spacers
- 4 in. (10cm) 24-gauge half-hard wire
- pair of decorative earring wires
- chainnose pliers
- roundnose pliers
- diagonal wire cutters

THE AMERICAS

The bead offerings of the Americas stretch from Canadian labradorite to Brazilian sodalite. Each region in between adds its own splash of color, including Mexican fire opals and brightly dyed Ecuadorian tagua beads. The Caribbean contributes texture with organic coconut beads, while clay beads from Peru, shaped like grasshoppers and painted by hand, add a bit of whimsy. Different areas of the United States have their own influences: the Native American squash-blossom design comes primarily from the Southwest, and the Great Lakes provide gently tumbled beach stones.

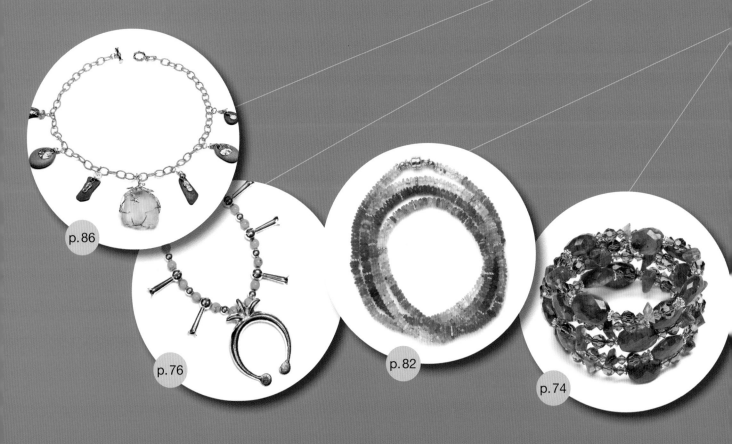

p.86

p.76

p.82

p.74

CANADA

GREAT
LAKES

SOUTHWESTERN
U.S.

MEXICO

CARIBBEAN

ECUADOR

PERU

BRAZIL

p.84

p.92

p.89

p.78

Encircle your wrist with a continuous strand of crystals and labradorite beads.

EDITOR'S TIP

When making a bracelet with nuggets, use a smaller-diameter (2-in./5cm) memory wire rather than bangle-sized wire. Heavier beads will stretch the wire's shape.

Make shimmering memory-wire cuffs with nuggets or chips from Labrador

by Naomi Fujimoto

Labradorite was named after the Canadian province where it was discovered. In the same family as moonstone, labradorite is often dark gray or greenish gray with a rainbowlike iridescence. To play up its shimmer, add crystals in shades of olive, teal, violet, or fuchsia. Both nuggets and chips lend themselves to easy wraparound bracelets.

SUPPLY LIST

nugget bracelet
- 16-in. (41cm) strand 12–15mm faceted labradorite nuggets
- **21–24** 6–8mm labradorite chips
- **42–48** 6mm round crystals, in two colors
- **84–96** 4mm bicone crystals
- **40–46** 4mm flat spacers
- memory wire, bracelet diameter (2 in./5cm)
- chainnose pliers or heavy-duty wire cutters
- roundnose pliers

chip bracelet
- 36-in. (.9m) strand 6–8mm labradorite chips
- **90–110** 4mm bicone crystals, in two colors
- memory wire, bracelet diameter (2 in./5cm or 2½ in./6.4cm)
- **2** 1½-in. (3.8cm) head pins
- chainnose pliers
- roundnose pliers
- diagonal wire cutters
- heavy-duty wire cutters (optional)

1 **nugget bracelet •** Separate the desired number of memory-wire coils from the stack, and add three coils. Cut the memory wire (see p. 81). Using roundnose pliers, make a small loop on one end.

2 String: bicone crystal, round crystal, bicone, chip, bicone, round, bicone, spacer, nugget, spacer. Repeat, alternating round-crystal colors, until the bracelet is the desired length.

3 Check the fit, and add or remove beads if necessary. Cut the memory wire ⅜ in. (1cm) from the last bead. Make a loop on the end of the wire.

1 **chip bracelet •** Separate the desired number of memory-wire coils from the stack, and add one coil. Cut the memory wire (see p. 81). Using roundnose pliers, make a small loop on one end.

2 String an alternating pattern of chips and crystals until the bracelet is the desired length. (If desired, string two or three chips between crystals.)

3 a Follow step 3 of the nugget bracelet.
b String two chips and a crystal on a head pin. Make the first half of a wrapped loop (Basics, p. 5). Repeat to make a second dangle.

4 Attach a dangle to each end loop, and complete the wraps.

The Zuni tribe added turquoise to the squash-blossom design, which was originally all silver.

The Native American squash-blossom design inspires a necklace-and-earring set

by Lindsay Haedt

Originally developed by the Navajo as an entirely silver jewelry piece, the squash-blossom necklace has evolved into a combination of silver and turquoise. The necklace featured here stays true to the original by including a naja pendant, a crescent-shaped decoration introduced in the Americas as a bridle ornament for Spanish conquistadors' horses. Traditional necklaces often contain elaborate metalwork with turquoise inlays.

1 **necklace •** Cut a piece of beading wire (Basics, p. 5). (This necklace is 16½ in./41.9cm.) On the wire, center a spacer, a naja pendant, and a spacer.

2 On each end, string a turquoise round bead, a silver round bead, a turquoise round, and a blossom bead. Repeat five times.

3 On each end, string a turquoise round and a silver round. Repeat until the strand is within 1 in. (2.5cm) of the desired length.

4 On each end, string a spacer, a crimp bead, a spacer, and half of a clasp. Check the fit, and add or remove beads from both ends if necessary. Go back through the beads just strung and tighten the wire. Crimp the crimp beads (Basics) and trim the excess wire.

INSPIRATION

Squash-blossom necklace and earrings from Albuquerque, New Mexico

1 **earrings •** On a head pin, string a turquoise round bead, a blossom tube bead, and a spacer. Make a wrapped loop (Basics).

2 Open the loop of an earring wire (Basics) and attach the dangle. Close the loop. Make a second earring to match the first.

SUPPLY LIST

Project materials are from Thunderbird Supply Company, (800) 545-7968, thunderbirdsupply.com.

necklace
- 40 x 54mm silver naja pendant
- **12** 25mm silver blossom beads
- 16-in. (41cm) strand 6mm round turquoise beads
- **20–30** 6mm round silver beads
- **6** 3mm round spacers
- flexible beading wire, .014 or .015
- **2** crimp beads
- toggle clasp
- chainnose or crimping pliers
- diagonal wire cutters

earrings
- **2** 16mm silver blossom tube beads
- **2** 6mm round turquoise beads
- **2** 3mm round spacers
- **2** 2-in. (5cm) head pins
- pair of earring wires
- chainnose pliers
- roundnose pliers
- diagonal wire cutters

Tagua products, like the beads that make this belt, provide a sustainable income for indigenous people of Ecuador without harming trees.

Beads made of nuts from South America are natural wonders

by Jane Konkel

Tagua (*tah-gwa*) nuts grow on palm trees in the tropical rain forests of South America. After the seedpods ripen and fall to the ground, harvesters dry them. The seeds are separated from their shells, cut into different shapes, polished, and dyed. Also called vegetable ivory, the natural color of tagua is white and resembles animal ivory.

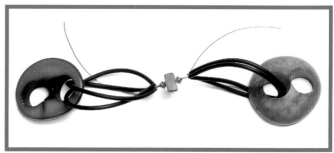

1 **belt** • To make a long rubber-and-tagua bead unit: Cut four 6-in. (15cm) pieces of rubber tubing and one 36-in. (.9m) piece of beading wire. String a crimp bead, a spacer, an irregular tagua bead, a spacer, and a crimp bead. Center the beads on the wire.

2 On one end, string a tube and one hole of a two-hole tagua bead. Go back through the crimp bead, spacer, irregular bead, spacer, and crimp bead. Repeat on the other end.

3 On each end, string a tube and the corresponding hole of the tagua bead. Go back through the crimp bead, spacer, irregular bead, spacer, and crimp bead. Tighten the wire, crimp the crimp beads (Basics, p. 5), and trim the excess wire.

4 Repeat steps 1, 2, and 3 to make three long tagua-and-rubber units.

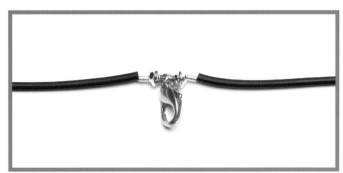

5 To make a connecting unit: Repeat step 1, substituting 5-in. (13cm) tubes for the 6-in. (15cm) tubes. Repeat step 2, stringing each remaining hole of two long tagua units. Connect the remaining long tagua unit with another connecting unit. Check the fit, allowing 3 in. (7.6cm) for finishing. Trim tubing if necessary. Tighten the wires, crimp the crimp beads, and trim the excess wires.

6 To finish: Cut two 2½-in. (6.4cm) pieces of rubber tubing and one 10-in. (25cm) piece of beading wire. On the wire, center: crimp bead, spacer, lobster claw clasp, spacer, crimp bead, tube.

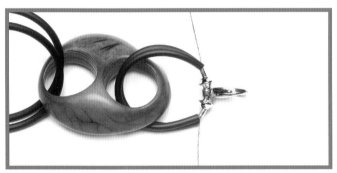

7 On one end, string each end of the wire, in opposite directions, through the remaining hole of a long tagua unit. Go back through the tube and the beads just strung. String the remaining tube and go back through the beads just strung.

SUPPLY LIST

belt
- **6** 40mm two-hole tagua beads, in a variety of colors (Acai Beads, 904-716-1061, acaibeads.com)
- **5** 10mm irregular tagua beads, in a variety of colors (Acai Beads)
- **12** large-hole spacers
- flexible beading wire, .018 or .019
- **4–5** ft. (1.2–1.5m) 2.5mm rubber tubing
- **13** large crimp beads
- 18mm lobster claw clasp
- Mighty crimping pliers
- diagonal wire cutters

bracelet
- **18–22** 10mm irregular tagua beads, in a variety of colors (Acai Beads)
- **18–22** large-hole spacers
- memory wire, bracelet diameter (2 in./5cm or 2½ in./6.4cm)
- **17–21** in. (43–53cm) 2.5mm rubber tubing
- **2** 1½-in. (3.8cm) decorative head pins
- chainnose pliers
- roundnose pliers
- diagonal wire cutters
- heavy-duty wire cutters (optional)

8 On the remaining end repeat steps 6 and 7, substituting a crimp bead for the beads strung. Tighten the wires, crimp the crimp beads, and trim the excess wire.

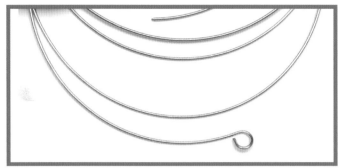

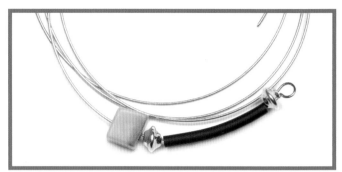

1 **bracelet** • Separate the desired number of memory-wire coils from the stack, and add three coils. Cut the memory wire (see tip below). Using roundnose pliers, make a small loop on one end (Basics).

2 Cut 17–21 1-in. (2.5cm) pieces of rubber tubing. String a spacer, a tube, a spacer, and an irregular tagua bead. Repeat, alternating tagua colors, until the bracelet is the desired length.

Check the fit, and add or remove beads and tubes if necessary. Cut memory wire ⅜ in. (1cm) from the last bead. Make a loop on the end of the wire.

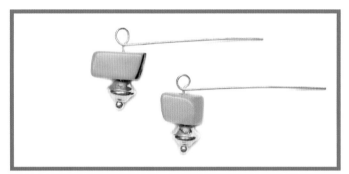

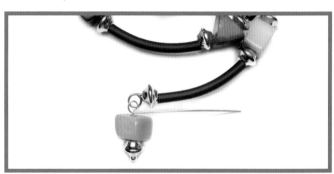

3 On a head pin, string a spacer and an irregular tagua bead. Make the first half of a wrapped loop (Basics). Make two bead units.

4 Attach a bead unit to each loop.

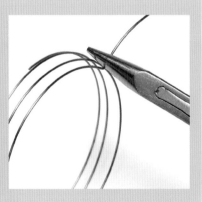

EDITOR'S TIP

To cut memory wire: Hold the wire with chainnose pliers and bend it back and forth at one place until the wire breaks. You also can use heavy-duty wire cutters. Do not use jewelry-weight wire cutters.

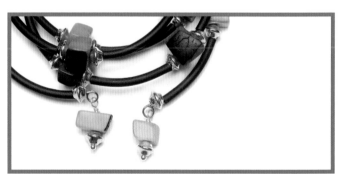

5 Complete the wraps.

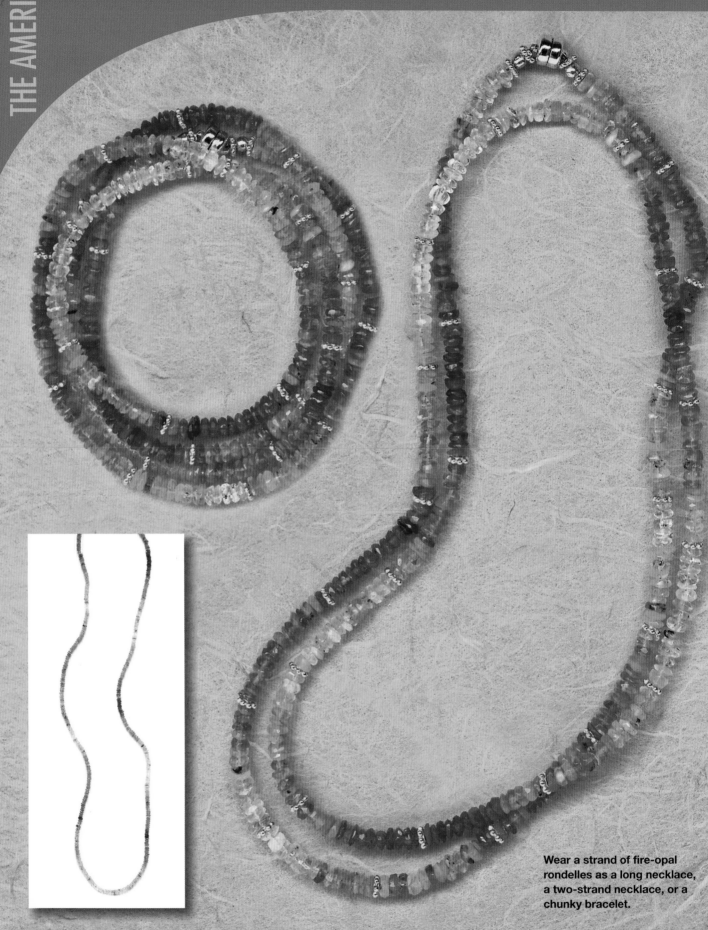

Wear a strand of fire-opal
rondelles as a long necklace,
a two-strand necklace, or a
chunky bracelet.

Showcase Mexican fire opals in a necklace that converts to a bracelet

by Lindsay Haedt

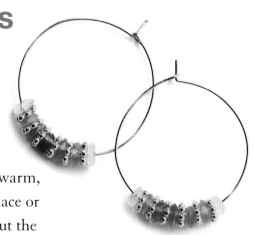

Mined in the highlands of Mexico, fire opals are renowned for their warm, rich colors. A long strand of faceted rondelles can be worn as a necklace or a bracelet, offering both style and versatility. Hoop earrings round out the ensemble, creating a sizzling look worthy of this fiery gemstone.

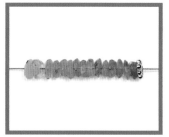

1 **necklace/bracelet** • Cut a piece of beading wire (Basics, p. 5). (This necklace/bracelet is 29 in./74cm.)
String 1 in. (2.5cm) of rondelles and a spacer. Repeat until the strand is within 1 in. (2.5cm) of the desired length. End with a rondelle.

2 On each end, string a spacer, a crimp bead, a spacer, and half of a clasp. Check the fit, and add or remove beads from both ends if necessary. Go back through the last few beads strung and tighten the wire. Crimp the crimp beads (Basics) and trim the excess wire. If desired, close a crimp cover over the crimp beads.

SUPPLY LIST

necklace/bracelet
- **2** 16-in. (41cm) strands 3–4mm faceted fire-opal rondelles (Rio Grande, 800-545-6566)
- **32–36** 4mm flat spacers
- flexible beading wire, .012 or .013
- **2** crimp beads
- **2** crimp covers (optional)
- magnetic clasp
- chainnose or crimping pliers
- diagonal wire cutters

earrings
- **14** 3–4mm faceted fire-opal rondelles (Rio Grande)
- **12** 4mm flat spacers
- 6 in. (15cm) 24-gauge half-hard wire
- chainnose pliers
- roundnose pliers
- diagonal wire cutters
- metal file or emery board
- empty spool

EDITOR'S TIP

To maintain the color pattern of the beads' gradation, place them in the channel of a bead design board before removing the string. Or transfer the beads directly from the string onto your beading wire.

1 **earrings** • Cut a 3-in. (7.6cm) piece of wire (Basics). Wrap it around an empty spool or other round object.

2 String an alternating pattern of seven rondelles and six spacers. Center the beads on the wire.

3 Approximately ⅛ in. (3mm) from one end, bend the wire up. File the end.

4 On the other end, make a plain loop (Basics). Make a second earring to match the first.

Coconut beads are lightweight, making them comfortable as well as stylish.

Capture the essence of the Caribbean with a coconut-and-coral necklace

by Lindsay Haedt

Originally from the western Pacific, coconuts now play both cultural and economic roles in many Caribbean nations. Synthetic apple coral adds a colorful contrast to the dark brown coconut and stays true to this necklace's tropical roots.

1 On a head pin, string a flower-shaped bead. Make a wrapped loop (Basics, p. 5). Make five flower-bead units.

2 Cut a piece of beading wire (Basics). (This necklace is 19 in./48cm.) Center a coconut bead, a flower-bead unit, and a coconut bead.

3 On each end, string a coral bead, a coconut bead, a flower-bead unit, and a coconut bead. Repeat.
On each end, string a coral bead and two coconut beads. Repeat until the strand is within 1 in. (2.5cm) of the desired length.

4 On each end, string a spacer, a crimp bead, a spacer, and half of a clasp. Check the fit, and add or remove beads from both ends if necessary. Go back through the beads just strung and tighten the wire. Crimp the crimp beads (Basics) and trim the excess wire.

SUPPLY NOTE

The orange-and-blue version of this necklace uses round metallic wood beads. The metallic wood beads, coconut flowers, and apple coral beads are available from Beads and Pieces, (800) 652-3237, or beadsandpieces.com.

SUPPLY LIST

- 5 30mm flower-shaped coconut beads
- 16-in. (41cm) strand 10mm round coconut beads
- 16-in. (41cm) strand 10mm round apple coral beads
- 4 3mm spacers
- flexible beading wire, .014 or .015
- 5 2-in. (5cm) head pins
- 2 crimp beads
- toggle clasp
- chainnose pliers
- crimping pliers (optional)
- roundnose pliers
- diagonal wire cutters

Beach-themed charms
and wire waves create
an aquatic motif.

Wire wrap a sea-glass necklace and earrings

by Jane Konkel

Sea glass comes from pieces of cast-off bottles worn smooth by the waves and sand and washed up on beaches. With the increasing use of plastic – and as littering becomes more and more discouraged – authentic sea glass is becoming difficult to find. Tumbled glass pieces are an alternative. Combine these smooth, elegant forms with beach stones that are sculpted by the wind, waves, and sand of the Great Lakes. Whether you comb the beach or collect rocks at the local craft store, this necklace-and-earring set will suit your seafaring fancy.

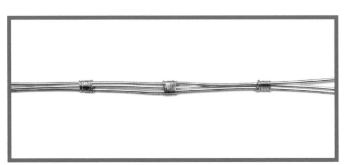

1 **necklace** • Cut three 9-in. (23cm) pieces of 22-gauge wire and three 3-in. (7.6cm) pieces of 26-gauge wire. Gather the 22-gauge wires. Wrap one 26-gauge wire around the center. Repeat on each side, approximately 1 in. (2.5cm) from the first set of wraps.

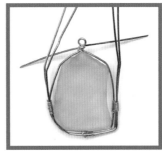

2 Form the wires around the sea-glass shard so the middle wrap is at the bottom. Bring the ends of the middle wire together, and make a wrapped loop (Basics, p. 5) above the pendant. Do not trim the tails.

3 Wrap each remaining wire once around the wraps.

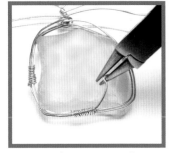

4 At each corner, on the front and back, use roundnose pliers to pull a wire toward the center of the shard. Leave the middle wire intact.

5 Grasp the end of each wire with the tip of your roundnose pliers and form a small loop. After a complete turn, reposition your pliers, and continue to form a spiral.

6 Hang the shard over the edge of a bench block. Hammer each spiral flat.

7 Press each spiral against the shard. Open a 3mm jump ring (Basics) and attach a charm and a wire. Close the jump ring.

Great Lakes

8 Cut a 4-in. (10cm) piece of 22-gauge wire. With the largest part of your roundnose pliers, make the first half of a wrapped loop. Do not trim the excess wire. Attach a beach stone, and complete the wraps.

9 **a** Use a 3mm jump ring to attach a charm to the wrapped loop.
  b Repeat steps 8 and 9a to make six to eight dangles.

10 Make a second wrapped loop above the first. Form a spiral with the wire that remains. Hammer the spiral as in step 6.

EDITOR'S TIP

To learn more about working with wire, check out *Inspired Wire*, by Cynthia Wuller, or *Art Jewelry* magazine, artjewelrymag.com.

11 Determine the finished length of your necklace. (This necklace is 17 in./43cm.) Cut a piece of chain to that length.
  Use a 5mm jump ring to attach the sea-glass pendant to the center link of chain. Use jump rings to attach the beach-stone dangles to the desired links. Check the fit, and trim chain from each end if necessary. Use 4mm jump rings to attach one half of a clasp to each end link.

earrings • Follow steps 8, 9a, and 10 of the necklace to make a beach-stone dangle. Open the loop of an earring wire (Basics) and attach the dangle. Close the loop. Make a second earring to match the first.

SUPPLY LIST

necklace
- sea-glass shard, approximately 40mm (Michaels, michaels.com for store locations)
- 6–8 16–28mm drilled beach stones (Riverstone Bead Company, 219-939-2050, riverstonebead.com)
- 7–9 8–12mm charms
- 4½–5 ft. (1.4–1.5m) 22-gauge dead-soft wire
- 9 in. (23cm) 26-gauge half-hard wire

- 16–19 in. (41–48cm) chain, 6–7mm links
- 7–9 5mm jump rings
- 2 4mm jump rings
- 7–9 3mm jump rings
- toggle clasp
- chainnose pliers
- roundnose pliers
- diagonal wire cutters
- bench block or anvil
- hammer

earrings
- 2 8–12mm drilled beach stones (Riverstone Bead Company)
- 2 8–12mm charms
- 8 in. (20cm) 22-gauge dead-soft wire
- 2 3mm jump rings
- pair of lever-back earring wires
- chainnose pliers
- roundnose pliers
- diagonal wire cutters
- bench block or anvil
- hammer

Brazil

Some crystal healers believe sodalite promotes inner peace.

Create a carnival of blue with Brazilian sodalite

by Tia Torhorst

Sodalite is named simply for its sodium content, but the look is anything but prosaic. The festive blues of this multistrand necklace and bracelet reflect the rich culture of Brazil.

1 necklace • a Cut a piece of beading wire for the shortest strand of your necklace (Basics, p. 5). (This one is 17½ in./ 44.5cm.) Cut two more pieces, each 3 in. (7.6cm) longer than the previous piece.

b Center a small briolette on the shortest wire. On each end, string five cylinder beads and a small briolette, repeating until the strand is within 1½ in. (3.8cm) of the desired length. On each end, string ¾ in. (1.9cm) of cylinders.

2 Center a medium briolette on the middle wire. On each end, string seven cylinders and a medium briolette, repeating until the strand is within 1½ in. (3.8cm) of the desired length.

On each end, string ¾ in. (1.9cm) of cylinders.

3 Center a large briolette on the longest wire. On each end, string nine cylinders and a large briolette, repeating until the strand is within 2 in. (5cm) of the desired length.

On each end, string 1 in. (2.5cm) of cylinders.

4 On each end of each strand, string a crimp bead and the corresponding loop of half of a clasp. Check the fit, and add or remove beads from both ends if necessary. Go back through the beads just strung and tighten the wire. Crimp the crimp beads (Basics) and trim the excess wire.

5 Using chainnose pliers, close a crimp cover over each crimp bead.

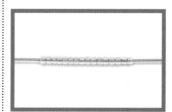

1 bracelet • Cut two pieces of beading wire (Basics). On one wire, center 16 cylinder beads.

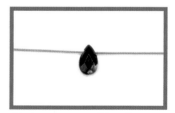

2 On each end, string a medium briolette, 16 cylinders, and a medium briolette. String cylinders until the strand is within 1 in. (2.5cm) of the desired length.

3 Center a small briolette on the second wire.

SUPPLY LIST

necklace
- **23–29** 12 x 18mm sodalite briolettes
- **29–35** 8 x 12mm sodalite briolettes
- **39–45** 6 x 8mm sodalite briolettes
- 5g 11º Japanese cylinder beads
- flexible beading wire, .014 or .015
- **6** crimp beads
- **6** crimp covers
- three-strand clasp
- chainnose pliers
- diagonal wire cutters
- crimping pliers (optional)

bracelet
- **4–8** 8 x 12mm sodalite briolettes
- **5–9** 6 x 8mm sodalite briolettes
- 1g 11º Japanese cylinder beads
- flexible beading wire, .014 or .015
- **4** crimp beads
- **4** crimp covers
- two-strand clasp
- chainnose pliers
- diagonal wire cutters
- crimping pliers (optional)

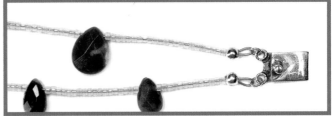

4 On each end, string 18 cylinders, a small briolette, 18 cylinders, and a small briolette. String cylinders until the strand is within 1 in. (2.5cm) of the desired length.

5 On each end of each wire, string a crimp bead and the corresponding loop of half of a clasp.

Check the fit, and add or remove beads from both ends if necessary. Go back through the beads just strung and tighten the wires. Crimp the crimp beads (Basics) and trim the excess wire.

Attach crimp covers as in step 5 of the necklace.

SUPPLY NOTE

Sodalite briolettes are available from Jade Mountain Bead & Jewelry Co. (608-256-5233) or Spacetrader Beads (spacetrader.com.au).

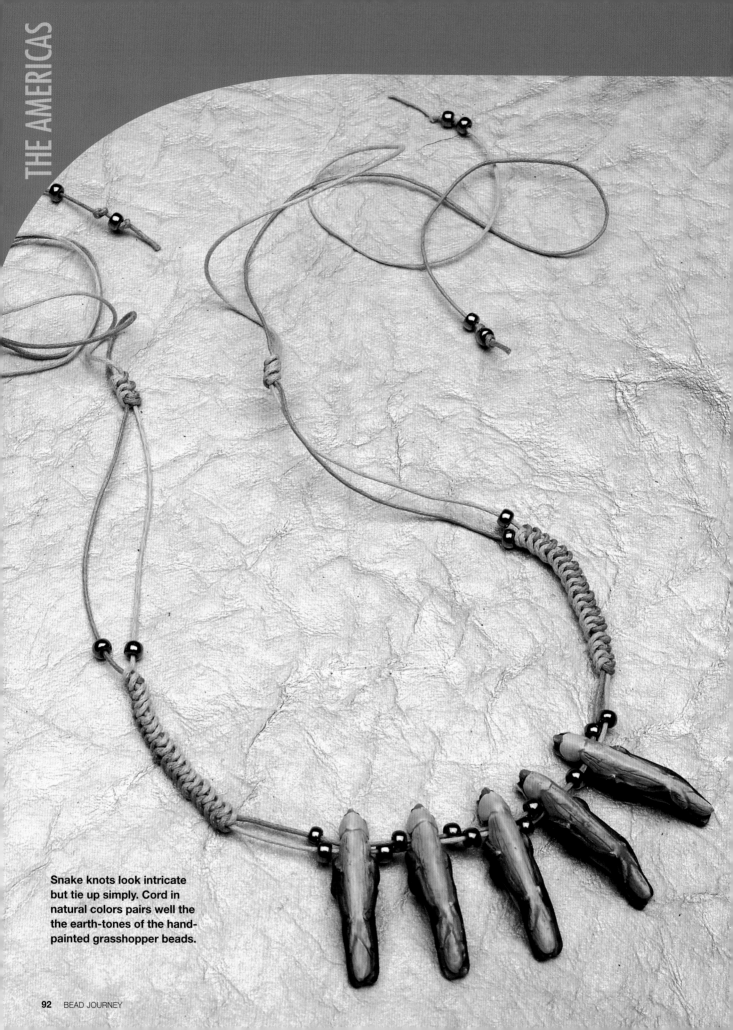

Snake knots look intricate but tie up simply. Cord in natural colors pairs well the the earth-tones of the hand-painted grasshopper beads.

Grasshopper beads and knotted cord give necklace an organic feel

by Jane Konkel

Hand-painted clay beads made in Peru pair naturally with thin cord. Tie snake knots in sections and add a few metallic seed beads to float along the cord. It's easy to be green with this down-to-earth, bib-style necklace.

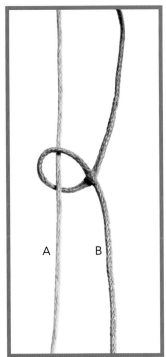

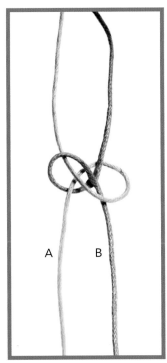

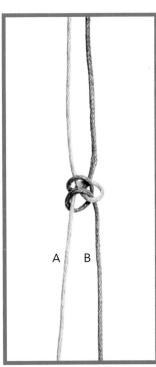

1 **a** Determine the finished length of your necklace. (This one is 3 ft./.9m.) Multiply that number by three, and cut two pieces of cord (one piece in each color) to that length. Approximately 15 in. (38cm) from one end, tie a snake knot with both cords.

b To tie a snake knot: String cord B under and over cord A, making a loop.

2 String A over B, then go back under B and through the first loop, making a loop with A. Pull both ends to loosely close the knot.

3 String B under A and down through A's loop. Pull B to loosely close the knot.

4 Turn the cords over. String A under B and down through the lower of the two loops. Pull cord A to loosely close the knot.

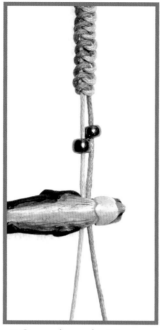

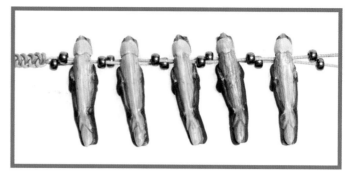

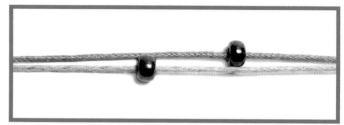

7 Repeat step 6, alternating pairs of 6°s and single grasshopper beads. End with a pair of 6°s.

5 Turn the cords back over, and repeat steps 3 and 4, tying snake knots to cover 1¾ in. (4.4cm) of the cords.

6 On each cord, string a 6° seed bead. Over both cords, string a grasshopper bead.

8 Approximately 4¼ in. (10.8cm) from the previous knot, repeat steps 1b through 5. On each end, over each cord, string a 6°.

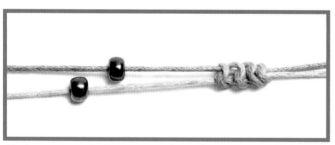

9 Approximately 3 in. (7.6cm) from the previous knot, repeat steps 1b through 4 with both cords. Turn the cords back over. Tie snake knots to cover ¼ in. (6mm) of the cords. Check the fit, allowing for the necklace to be tied, and trim cord from each end if necessary. String a 6° on each cord. Repeat on the other end.

SUPPLY LIST

- **5** grasshopper beads (JP Imported, 707-541-0301, jpimported.com)
- **24** 6° seed beads
- 8–10 ft. (2.4–3m) 5mm round cord, color A
- 8–10 ft. (2.4–3m) 5mm round cord, color B

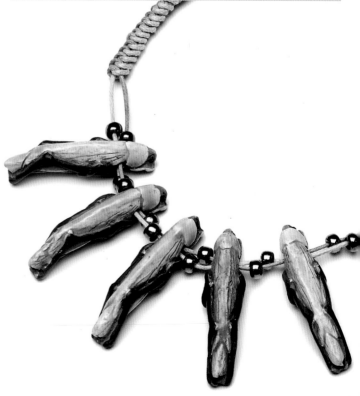

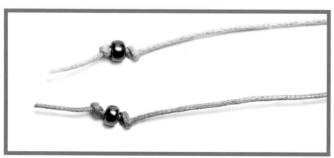

10 Approximately 1 in. (2.5cm) from each end of each cord, tie an overhand knot (Basics, p. 5). String a 6°, and tie an overhand knot. Repeat on the other end.

Contributors

Linda Augsburg is Senior Editor/Online for *BeadStyle*, *Bead&Button*, and *Art Jewelry* magazines. Contact her through Kalmbach Books.

Michael Bellomo is an avid art history buff, amateur gemologist, and all-around rockhound, which aids and abets his hobby as a jewelry artist based out of Los Angeles, Calif. Contact him via e-mail at ghostrh@hotmail.com.

Melanie Ehler is a writer, dancer, and commissioned jewelry designer. Contact her via e-mail at melindyhop@yahoo.com.

Naomi Fujimoto is Senior Editor of *BeadStyle* magazine and the author of *Cool Jewels: Beading Projects for Teens*. Contact her through *BeadStyle*.

Formerly Editorial Associate of *BeadStyle,* **Lindsay Haedt** is currently pursuing a teaching degree. Contact her through the magazine.

Cathy Jakicic is Editor of *BeadStyle*. Contact her through the magazine.

Jane Konkel is Associate Editor of *BeadStyle*. Contact her through the magazine.

Although **Marichelle Limjuco-Lopez** stays busy as the full-time mother of a baby boy, she still finds time to make personalized beaded jewelry designs. Contact Marichelle at Efarca Village, Schetelig Ave., 4000 San Pablo City, Laguna, Philippines, or via e-mail at mlimjuco@yahoo.com.

Contact **Andrea Loss** via e-mail at amloss@wi.rr.com.

Washington D.C. artist and activist **Tia Torhorst** likes to create, whether it's making funky jewelry, knitted treasures, and paper crafts, or growing veggies in her urban garden. Contact her via e-mail at tiatorhorst@yahoo.com or via her Web site, tiatorhorst.com.

Heart

Square

Round

V-neck

Turtleneck

FLATTERY IS JUST A FASHIONABLE PROJECT AWAY!

Complement what you look like and what you're wearing with jewelry made for it! With more than 30 informative and imaginative projects, you'll be able to create the length, shape, and size jewelry that will best match the features of your face and your garment necklines. 96 pages.

62618 • $19.95

BeadStyle BOOKS

JEWELRY JUST FOR YOU!

Projects that flatter every face shape and neckline

round face heart-shaped face oval face square
eck strapless round neckline turtleneck v-neck

Oval

Strapless

Check out these other cool guides to great looks for every day of the year!

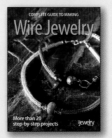
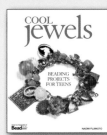

Order online at www.BeadAndCraftBooks.com or call 1-800-533-6644

Monday–Friday, 8:30 a.m.–5:00 p.m. Central Time. Outside the U.S. and Canada, call 262-796-8776 x661.

BeadStyle BOOKS